THE LONG ROAD HOME
A JOURNAL OF A JOURNEY ECLIPSED

DAVID BROWN

Copyright © 2021 David Brown

All rights reserved.

ISBN: 978-1-7367648-0-0

This book is dedicated to my daughter whose love fuels me to continue on. The patience and support you show helps guide me on my journey. I can only hope to bring you the amount of peace and joy you bring me.
To the moon and back chicken.

CONTENTS

Introduction - 1

Chapter One - 3

Chapter Two - 8

Chapter Three - 14

Chapter Four - 21

Chapter Five - 30

The Light to Paradise - 40

Chapter Seven - 52

Chapter Eight - 64

Chapter Nine - 71

Introduction

Understanding and Reason

Thanks for opening up the book and indulging to read my pages in history as I stumble along the path and over words. Here is a little understanding of who I am and a reason for how this all came about. Or maybe it's an understanding of how this came about and a reason for who I am. Either way here we are.

When I came to this realm I was gifted the name of David. I was born in Ohio and have been here my entire life. I'm currently in the southeastern end of the state, near Dayton. A lot of people talk bad about Ohio but really it's a great spot. The scenery is not overly beautiful - allowing proper desire to travel and explore the world - and the beautiful souls that fill it beckon you home. I remember going on hikes in nature through state and national parks as a kid. They would end up being the moments that initially kindled the internal fire of adventure. A trip to Germany with the student exchange program as a teen essentially tossed a log that would never fully burn down on that fire. Throughout adolescence and into my early adult life my travel consisted mainly of me tagging along with my family to North Carolina, Florida, and Michigan. Trips either to the beach or to go see family. I would always find time to explore the area around me. The circumference of exploration grew as I did. Traveling was initially a method of temporary escape from a life I was not very content with. As I grew and fell more in love with my self I would shift the focus of my travels to explorations in beauty. Moving with the intention of finding the light in the world and sharing my light in an attempt to find where the two converge.

Throughout my journey I have felt a connection to The Universe.

David Brown

When I take the time to step back for a moment I get a glimpse in time to watch how the puzzle pieces fell into place. The language used is seldom spoken words. Rather the moments, in whole, are generally used as language to speak to us. Synchronicities and things that seem like coincidence are used as guiding lights along on the path. My journeys are spiritual in nature - ventures both in and out. I am pulled by The Universal Force and led by spirit. My heart of hearts connects with this force though intuition. This is about the time the universal winds took me to Wyoming to witness a solar eclipse in totality.

The idea for this book came about after the trip, once I soaked in the energy for a few months. I have wanted to be a writer since I was young. It has always been my favorite form to get my feelings and ideas out. I remember the first time I wrote anything was in kindergarten or first grade. We wrote a short story, mine was about a wizard and had the moral of acceptance. Our teacher laminated and bound them for us. Looking back I find peace with the fact that during that time in my life, a fairly dark period after my parents divorce, I still chose to write about acceptance. I realized while writing that short story that I wanted to write as an adult. This was a pretty easy way to get started in the art of writing, allowing me to get my wrist loose per se. It is essentially a journal about my road trip to Wyoming for a solar eclipse. I intended to fill the pages with moments I felt were magical. I've sprinkled in bits of knowledge I have been gifted along my journey that have helped me garner peace, love, and joy. My hopes is someone else will find this helpful.

I wish you all much love, peace, and strength along our journey. I hope you take the time to stop and smell the flowers, listen to the birds, or watch the sun come and go. Until our paths cross.

CHAPTER ONE

A Total Soular Eclipse

Driving east through Nebraska I had just passed mile marker 210 as I glanced over at the clock on the dashboard. The burning red display etched the 3:00 into my mind. Reminding me how far away the morning sun was, even as I raced toward it. A few moments later I would pass what would seem to be The Universe beckoning me with a sign - a "Rest Area One Mile Ahead" sign to be exact. I had been hoping to find the sunrise as I had surmised the light would help me fight fatigue to extend my journey - in a rush to get to my destination. I had driven over 4,500 miles in a little over a week meandering across the country on a adventure filled with hiking, backpacking, camping, and most of all love. I had driven to Wyoming for the eclipse and then up to Grand Teton National Park. I was on the last leg of my journey, headed toward what turned out to be my most prized destination - home with my daughter. I was in a rush to get back but after the sun set the darkness drew my eyelids closer to their darkness. I was exhausted after being up for over twenty hours with hiking followed by driving. My personal fuel reserves were draining faster than my vehicles. All the signs led me to surrender to sleep.

I have found that the mistakes in life are made when I get into a rush. My patience dwindles and I lose sight of what is. The Universe has been dealing me the lesson that patience is the key to everything recently. I am finding that rushing will not get you anything faster, and in fact might cause you to miss some of the magical things being offered to you. If nothing else having the patience to let the storm pass allows you to find your center amid the chaos, allowing you to move in more clarity. It's a constant practice.

My eyes were getting heavy like the clouds as the thunderstorm rolls in. My eye lids seemed to be closing in on the horizon in much the same way the clouds do as they build. We had been up since seven in the morning to do a hike up to Hidden Falls in Grand Teton National Park. After which I packed camp before we celebrated the trip one last time together. I was on the road just before five that evening.

As I laid my seat back and nestled my head as comfortably on the head rest as feasible my mind began to drift between thoughts. I was back to the moments the trip first began and the excitement that came with going west of Chicago for the first time. The only night I had planned other than meeting up with Andrew and the gang was the first night at Perrot State Park in Trempealeau, Wisconsin. I had a campsite reserved right on The Mississippi River. To add to the excitement I would be catching the Total Solar Eclipse of 2017 on the side of a mountain in Wyoming, in totality and relative seclusion. The excitement had been building over roughly a years time for this trip, from the moment Andrew first started researching the idea and offered me the opportunity of a lifetime. It only grew the more research he did and the more we narrowed in on plans. I had about 8 months of building anticipation from the moment we finalized our plans. Andrew, being the resourceful researcher of the group, did all the planning and mapping. We could of caught totality much closer to our home in Dayton, Ohio, but we all desired a more secluded experience to this once in a lifetime event. Andrew, his girlfriend Maranda, and our buddy Rob all decided to fly over to Denver and catch a concert at Red Rocks before driving up to Wyoming. I passed on the plane ticket for the more adventurous route of driving over. I had never been west of Chicago and had a desire to experience as much as there was to offer along the way. I would embark on a wayward journey west to Dubois, Wyoming.

I hoped to spread my love, appreciation, and gratitude with everything I encountered along the way. To radiate it let it ripple around me and reverberate back at me. There is a countless number of beautiful souls and scenes I had never experienced. I would go off in search of as many as I could find on my way to Wyoming. It was my chance to relinquish my fears and let go. An opportunity to open my heart and begin to follow the path that starts at its gate. To make music with The Universe and dance with it. In order to dance with The Universe you must move in love and relinquish all fears and judgement so I made that my focus.

The Long Road Home

Initially I had hoped to take my nine year old daughter on the journey. After discussing with her mother we decided against that idea since her first day of school was the day I was leaving. It tore my heart apart but I tried to focus on what the lesson was in the moment. I have adopted the idea that there is a lesson in everything in life. Omnia causa fiunt - everything happens for a reason. The lesson present here was not immediately clear to me but it would become more apparent along the way that I needed this journey for my self, as a spiritual journey inward. I had no idea I would be exploring the depths of my self more deeply the further away I got. I was going to rediscover my light as much as I was going to witness the moon cast its shadow over the solar light. We can recreate the journey and go even further when the time is right.

This journey has was the fruition of me concentrating on giving my self as much time as I give my career in life. It all began when I lost my job at Redbox a few years prior. I had lost the job due to a seat belt violation that occurred off work time a year prior that I did not file with Human Resources. I had worked there for over seven years. And had for much of that time dedicated upwards of 80 hours a week to them, though towards the end it had leveled out to a little over 40 hours a week. I had dedicated a majority of my time to them believing that I was doing what was best for my family, though I had been slightly misguided by that idea as I would come to learn. My mother and father were both victims of less than desirable employers. They had dedicated their life to companies and been given less than their fair shake in the end. They had very little to show for their years of dedication. So I had seen this idea of dedicating all your time to your career not being a great investment before but among the chaos of being a new dad and a fear of not being able to provide I dismissed these things. The Universe had whispered to me initially that it was my time to go a few years prior to losing my job but I dismissed the whisper due my fears as well as a lack of confidence in The Universe or my self. The whispers would get louder and louder, each time I would shake them off, each time they came back more vigorously. Until finally I had a fender bender off work time that I filed with HR. At which time they pulled a motor vehicle report and noticed the seat belt violation. It pushed me over their metrics for being a driver and due to corporate standards they were forced to let me go. The universe decided to start speaking a little more clearly to me, realizing that I wasn't moving due to fear. The greatest failure we can experience in life is the inaction caused by fear.

   Introspectively my fears seemed well founded, I had a family to provide for and Redbox was all I had known for that duty. But anytime you don't trust The Universe and your connection to it, through intuition, your fears are not rational and should be examined. I had been offered the job at approximately the same time I found out I was going to be a father - the timing of The Universe is always magical. It was a job that provided fairly well for my family and wasn't overly stressing. They had blessed me with some great opportunities in life. They offered me the opportunity to take time away, on short notice, while I sat by my grandmothers bedside in Hospice through her last days in this body. I was able to be with her through her last moments here and hold her hand as she entered the next realm of life. I still don't know that she has let go of my hand, which brings me peace. I was not confident in my ability to do what I had dreamed or what the universe had planned. I was being given the opportunity to examine those fears and face them head on - when you face your fears head on, with your light, you'll notice they just dissipate.

   Since losing my job I had finished my associated degree at the local community college in Science of Biology. Through college I had found the experiences with my peers and professors more profound than anything they would test me on toward the degree. After school I had worked a few frivolous jobs, usually for a year a piece. I would move on when I felt my time up or heard the universe beckoning me out. I was working a job at a local nursery doing maintenance of the grounds, part-time at a low rate of pay. I left with about 450 dollars in my pocket and the expectation of getting a two week check of 27 hours at 10 dollars per hour the Friday after I left. A chance for me to put my fears of "not enough" out of mind and trust in the plan of The Universe. The experiences I was after were priceless anyhow. I was spreading my wings and riding The Universal Wind.

   From a young age I have felt pulled from forces both inside and outside of myself. Like I was being pulled to something bigger than myself. I remember having the idea at a very early age that dreams and "awake realities" were fairly interchangeable. Perhaps when we were dreaming was actually the reality and so when we were awake perhaps that was the time that we were dreaming. It would shatter my idea of reality. My imagination never helped hold the reality together very well in the first place. I think that was the initial switch into my journey into consciousness, although the path was sketchy at the beginning. When I was young I had idea that I was meant for great things. Back then my ideas of great were what you would expect from someone young; money, fame, and power. The further down the path I get I realize this greatness to often be obtained in the minuscule moments that grow out into greatness., like ripples in a pond. You don't need to throw a boulder to cause a movement, even a small stone will cause a wave.

This was my chance to spread my wings after breaking the cocoon that I had metaphorically built and rested in for some time. I would ride the wind that had sustained my breath since the beginning of time. I was finding my self in harmony with The Universe, and in the winds that carry me. They are one in the same.

As I slowed down my mind and focused on my breath as it moved through the body I slowly drifted off to the land of dreams. I have always been intrigued by the fact that in dreams I have as much of an idea of what another person is thinking as I do in reality.

Hold your light through the storm and once it passes the two will create the rainbow. You will never see the beauty of the rainbow if you do not hold your light.

CHAPTER TWO

Waywardly Wandering West

Day One: 08/16/2017

I woke up around five in the morning, a rare occasion of waking up before the alarm. Even through the excitement of the trip I slept soundly and was up ready to get my day started. The trip had been on my mind for the past week, almost constantly. The excitement was building up over the past six or so months before finally peaking over the last week. I might of had everything packed a week ahead of time had I not needed things between then and leaving. I packed my bags the night before and sat them by the door in an attempt to streamline my exit. I double checked my list and squeezed my gear into the CR-V like a Tetris great as I brewed some coffee. After letting my family know I was getting on the road and giving my love I filled my thermos with coffee and headed out the door. I had a full tank of gas and clean windows thanks to a premeditated stop the night before to the gas station. Everything was bursting full; my CR-V with supplies and gas, my thermos with coffee, and my self with excitement. The tires were rolling and I was moving down the road on a journey I could hardly begin to fathom.

    I would head over to see my daughter off on her first day of school from her mothers house. As much as I wanted to see her before her first day of school, seeing her made it difficult to know she wasn't going on this trip. Knowing I would not see her for another week brought feelings of sadness bubbling to the surface from below a froth of excitement. After getting some pictures and giving some love she hopped on the bus and I was back behind the wheel. I made one last stop at the gas station on my way to the interstate for some coffee and ice for the cooler. I got two bags of ice and a cup of coffee which came to $7.77. A laugh roared up from my belly and told the cashier that I had already hit the jackpot. Just another sign from The Universe that I was on the right path. I've always looked for synchronistic bubbles popping around me as signs that I am strolling the right direction on this journey. Some may dismiss them as coincidences, but I have never been much a fan of those.

Traffic ran smoothly along the highway as I traveled west then northwest through Indiana and Illinois. It started to rain intermittently as I traversed north through Illinois. My mind began to drift as it transitioned to a steady pace on the windshield with the wipers clapping in time. My mind seemed to teeter between thoughts of my daughter - the sadness that she couldn't come with - and daydreams of what the future days would hold. The swinging of the pendulum of thoughts between my daughter and the adventure was constantly interrupted with the joy of enjoying the moment as I moved through new experiences. The landscape around me, even through the dreary weather was still beautiful and mystifying. My excitement was growing to reach the Mississippi River with each shift in landscape.

Wisconsin would offer a whole new shift in experiences. The weather shifted from overcast to partly cloudy before finally letting the sun break out a majority of the time. Only interrupted by the occasional cloud moving across the sky. It was a refreshing change and made the beauty Wisconsin holds radiate in the fresh light. This was the one night I had planned before meeting up with the gang in Wyoming, and I would be staying along the Mississippi River in the beautiful town of Trempealeau, Wisconsin. The scenery was beautiful in Wisconsin, even from the highway. As I wandered my way down the road my mind was lost taking in the scenery and I missed my turn onto a small highway. I decided to take the next turn and exchange my highway drive for a pleasant drive down a country road as an alternate route for a bit. It would end up being one of the better decisions I had made as the road took me on a beautiful backroad. It wound through Wisconsin country side through rolling hills and across small, rolling streams. Dairy farms dotted the country side like the spots on the cows that they housed. The bright red barns stuck out against the bright green fields and hills. With each farm I passed I was desiring some fresh Wisconsin cheese more and more until around one of the bends in the road I passed a small shop called The Hyde Store. Instantly knowing I had just passed my possibility for some fresh cheese I turned around at the next country road and headed back to find a parking spot. It wasn't terribly hard as there were maybe three cars in the gravel lot that was overtaken by grass.

    I parked the car and headed up to the store to get some local cheese and any other treats they may offer up. I was almost shaking with the excitement of holding some delicious cheese in my hand as I walked toward the door. As I opened the door and walked through time seemed to stop. If there would have been a record playing it would have stopped. Everyone turned around to see who walked through the door, I'm sure expecting to greet a fellow local. Mind you I'm an early 30's, skinny, hippie looking character - definitely not of the local cast of characters.. My hair was roughly shoulder length, dreaded - not clean dreads either but natural, nappy dreads - with a buff (similar to a bandana but a continuous tube of stretchy material) holding it out of my face. I don't know that many of the locals familiarize with the style. I'm in the middle of dairy county and The Hyde Store is not a store at all, but a small, hole in the wall, local bar. It was all of a bar that took up the entire side of one end of the bar. It had maybe 9 stools, all filled with a local gentlemen. A kind old lady, probably the wife of one of the men if I had to guess, was behind the bar serving the beer. I broke the ice, offering the only explanation I had,"Hello, I'm not from around here, obviously. " I paused my explanation as the small room erupt in laughter. I finished explaining that I was passing through and noticed the store and hoped to get some local cheese, but obviously this isn't the kind of store I imagined, and I doubt I'll find any cheese. Everyone in the bar broke out in joyous laughter again. The gentleman at the end of the bar offered up where I would be able to get some local cheese, and pointed me toward Arena Cheese down the road. I offered to refresh his beer to which he hesitantly accepted. I told him at the very least it would make all the other guys wish they had spoke up and offered directions. I believe after tipping the bar lady a couple dollars for her troubles my total was five dollars. I offered up my love and appreciation to everyone as I turned around and headed out the door, basking in the glory of that random moment of joy. I was not even a day into my journey and I had already been offered a random opportunity from The Universe to spread some joy and love with random, beautiful souls. I hopped back into my car and followed the directions of my friend from the bar to Arena Cheese.

    After roughly fifteen minutes of driving through beautiful Wisconsin country side I turned onto a small highway and noticed my destination roughly a quarter of a mile down the road on the left. The statue of a mouse waving with a brick of cheese out front. The mouse stood below a big red sign with white letters stood out fairly well. I parked the 4 wheeled steed and headed in to grab some Wisconsin cheese. I also found some beef sausage snack links in a cooler near the cheddar cheese. As I made my way to the register a ten foot long section of white metal store shelves filled top to bottom with local jellies, jams, and preservatives caught my attention. I glanced them over and settled on strawberry jelly amongst the many other fruit varieties. I shared a smile with the cashier as I thanked her with love and appreciation as I headed out the door back toward my final destination for the day. I snapped a couple tourist- type photos with the mouse and me before refilling my coffee cup, pouring some tea, and getting back behind the wheel. It had been roughly an eight hour day already, but I was feeling refreshed. I was heading toward Trempealeau but had plans to swing through Wisconsin Dells to check it out on recommendation of my friend. I was hoping I would find some food while there before embarking the rest of the way to my campsite.

As I pulled into the Dells I realized immediately it was not where I wanted to be. It reminded me of the Wisconsin version of Gatlinburg, Tennessee, and I've just never much enjoyed it there. My hopes of finding a spot to get some food were also dwindling, I am sure if I would of searched I could of found something, but I was feeling pulled to move on. I found the nearest available option to turn around and reversed course.

Pulling into Trempealeau just before dark I had still not stopped for food so I made that a priority above setting up camp. Searching town I stumbled upon The Historic Trempealeau Inn and stopped in for some food. I was offered a seat on the porch overlooking the river and graciously accepted the beautiful view. I ordered up a local Angus beef hamburger and some delicious sweet potato fries. After finishing my meal I decided to grab a beer, something I don't do very often, to celebrate. I headed out on the deck to soak in the views and the moment. After finishing my beer and paying I was headed toward the door when one of the owners, who was sitting in the lobby finishing some work, stopped me and asked how everything was. After a few minutes she offered up that I go upstairs and check out one of the empty rooms if I liked. The rooms were beautiful, traditional rooms with a beds of the same era of the hotel, with updated mattresses, and shared bathroom spaces in the hallway. The whole place held a very homely feeling and I knew this was where my daughter and I would stay when we recreated the trip together. I headed back downstairs toward the door and thanked the kind co-owner for letting me check out the space and assured her I would be booking a room when we headed back. I was off to my campsite and a good nights rest, finally.

I headed down the road along the river toward Perrot State Park where I was camping for the night. When I pulled into the park it was just beginning to sprinkle. I headed cautiously down the road making careful effort to read the signs holding directions to the various campsite numbers through the rain and dark. I wound around and found my camp spot and backed in, deciding against setting up my tent as it was already late and raining. I had not planned to stay too late into the morning anyhow to justify putting it up and down. I would spend my first night on the journey sleeping in the back seat of my car, unable to fully stretch out.

Before heading to bed, and as uncomfortable as it seemed it was calling my name, I headed down by the river at my site to sit and take a couple puffs off the pipe while I sat back and soaked in the moment and joy of being on this adventure. As I sat there meditating, occasionally taking a pull from the pipe, my mind fluttered between envisioning my life; where I was going, where I had been, but most importantly where I am now. I thought of all the amazing and beautiful people I had met and would meet along the way, and the amazing and beautiful person I was in the process of meeting right here and now.

Years ago I would not have been wanting to sit here with my self. I was not comfortable in my own skin, perhaps because I did not see or realize my own light. It is quite the journey through some dark spots to find our light and radiate it. I was just beginning to break my shell, and coming out of the dark, sometime it takes some time to fully adjust to the light.

It began to rain a little steadier, but not enough to drown the fire I was stoking within my self. After some time I decided to relinquish the self from the realm of this reality to the realm of the dream reality and headed toward bed, my car. Laying down I realized I had a slight tilt to my mind, the beer I had hit me a little more than I anticipated it would, paired with cannabis probably helped. I never know what to expect since I only drink a few times a year. This seemed like the perfect opportunity though - a celebration of embarking on the journey

The Long Road Home

of a lifetime. As I closed my eyes I heard some rumbles of thunder off in the distance, I would be blessed with a night of sleeping through storms.

You will exert less energy if you can let the universe pull you where you are needed as opposed to pushing for where you want to go. Plus the journey will be more rewarding as well.

CHAPTER THREE

Across the Mighty River

Day Two: 08/17/2017

After a restless night of sleep I woke up around five in the morning, oddly enough well rested, with the sun still under the horizon. The last efforts of the storms from last night were still present as it rained lightly, the sky was still dark as I climbed out of the back seat to go relieve myself near a tree. I brewed some coffee on the backpacking stove while I ate a bowl of cereal before getting back on the road. Just as I was leaving the park grounds the sun was starting to make it's way over the horizon. The storm had moved out enough to allow for a beautiful sunrise. The remaining clouds from the storm added depth and beauty to the painting. The sky filled with oranges, then red, then pink with each inch the sun seemed to peak over the horizon until it finally burned them all off. The rain broke after about an hour or so to complete sunshine, it would be the last rain clouds I would see the whole trip. The heavens opens up above me just as I was about to cross The Mississippi.

    Just before reaching the river I stopped for gas and grabbed a cup of coffee. I used the time to scan the road atlas for todays destination. As my eyes scanned the map for clumps of green, generally indicative of forest or parks, I kept being pulled toward Big Sioux Recreation Area just across the South Dakota border, in the small town of Brandon, South Dakota. Researching what amenities it offered I realized it was the right move. They offered camping, hiking, and disc golf. I had packed my discs just in case I might stumble on somewhere to play and I was pretty happy with that decision now. More importantly, after over ten hours of driving yesterday, it was a short eight hour

The Long Road Home

journey.

For some reason the route my GPS used took me across The Mississippi three times. It took me across to Iowa, back to Wisconsin, and back across to Iowa and jettisoned me off west. I have always been intrigued by math and numbers, from a very young age they spoke to me and I understood them. As I have moved through life I have use numbers as a language to communicate with The Universe. Three has always seemed tied to me and has always been one of my favorite numbers, I would see it pop up throughout life. In college my study of mathematics led me to the magic of the numbers three, six, and nine. Something Nikola Tesla spoke on as well. Here was just another moment I felt The Universe speak to me in numbers - carrots of reassurance that the path I was treading was a proper path.

I headed through the northeast corner of Iowa across southern Minnesota. The drive across southern Minnesota was an uneventful drive along the highway. Just me on the open road, with a few cars here or there, music playing and windows open. The sun was radiating down as it hung in a clear blue sky. Other than stopping for gas and coffee my wheels continued to turn, like my mind. I meandered down the road as I headed west and crossed into South Dakota. I was beginning to tune into the music of The Universe and losing myself in the dance. The beauty of the west was unreal to me, even this early on. The line between reality and dream was beginning to evanesce.

Pulling in to the park I stopped by the ranger station and picked out a campsite. The little shed style offie was empty so I filled out my registration and left it there. I would have to come back later grab some wood and pay for the campsite. I wound my way down the park road to find my campsite, it was just after two in the afternoon and the weather was beautiful. I quickly found my site and was pleased that there were no other camps set up within a thousand feet of my site. I picked a spot on the site I thought my tent might get some evening shade and had it set up in roughly ten minutes. After getting my tent up I headed over to some shade with some tea and my book and set up my chair. Birds were singing their beautiful praise as I relaxed in the shade, immersed in the book I was reading. Once I finished the chapter I was on I decided to take advantage of the beautiful day and head to the disc golf course.

The course was designed and set up beautifully. It meandered through the woods and along the Big Sioux River with holes sprinkled in among the meadows and trees. A majority of the trees in the woods were old, gnarly trees with trunk and branches twisted in various ways. A few young ones filled in where they could. When I am in the presence of trees, especially old trees, I wonder what they have been through or witnessed - especially when they have a big old knot or crazy bend. It seemed as though I had the entire place to myself. Other than a local gentleman walking his dog, who stopped for a brief conversation, I only noticed a handful of people. After nearly losing two disc I headed back to camp. I decided on the walk back to camp to set my sleep system up and go grab some fire wood. I also decided tonight was a good night for a couple of the hotdogs I had brought in the cooler. I would cook them over the fire, with s'mores for desert. A family of three from Minnesota, based on their license plate, were setting up camp and unloading amenities from their Subaru. For the time being we just exchanged brief pleasantries on my way over to the park office to grab some firewood.

After I acquired my fire wood for the night I headed back to my chair in the shade with my book and some tea to relax for another hour or so. Finishing another chapter in the book I decided that it was about perfect time to hike around and hopefully find a good spot to see the sunset. While playing disc golf I noticed a foot bridge that went across the river following a path that led up a hill. I tossed a couple snacks and a drink into my backpack and put my boots on to head off again on an adventure.

The park offered a nice set of paved paths for walking or biking that ran around the entire perimeter of the park and cut through in various spots. Dirt paths cut through and offered a more secluded hike here and there. I noticed an eagle flying over as I was headed to the bridge I spotted earlier and couldn't help but imagine what his view was like. I imagine the park looked like a spiderweb of paths laid over the green of the grass and trees with the river cutting through and hills just on the other side of the river. I headed toward the golf holes that ran along the water to find the bridge that led across the river to the hills. Along the river there were a dozen or so turtles soaking up the early-evening sun along the opposite shore. I was excited to see what else was ahead for me.

I headed over the bridge and down the path toward the hill. As I approached the hill I was confronted with a crossroads of paths with a signpost holding a map. There was another set of spiderweb paths running on this side of the river, this one traversing meadows and hills

The Long Road Home

which seemed to offer up some overlooks. I chose the path that seemed to take me to the highest point hoping to find some nice views from above. Just after I started down the path there was an archery range off to the left. Nobody was shooting now so I looked around before heading up the hill. Various birds were serenading me with their beautiful songs along the way and I had various encounters, all friendly, with some bees, butterflies, and bunnies. Other than my nature friends I only passed one hiker and a mountain biker who crossed paths with me a few times. I was noticing an abundance of beauty, which seemed to be presenting itself, both for me and with me, along this strange path of life I was on. When I reached the top of the hills, before the path gradually led down the other side, I stopped to take in the views and relax for a bit. I had come on this adventure to get high and see the views - speaking of which I was ready for a couple pulls from the pipe.

Off the trail to the left, maybe fifteen feet from the trail there was a big rock sticking maybe three feet out of the ground roughly six feet across at its widest point. It was sitting under the shade of some trees at the top of the hill - a perfect seat that felt like it was placed here just for me. Sitting atop the hill soaking in the sights I would occasionally soak in the spirits of cannabis as well. Cannabis has always been a very spiritual medicine for me, often enhancing and showing me the connection between things that seem to make up our world - be it other people, animals or any other aspect of life. I have felt a connection along this journey so far.

My eyes roved as well as my mind as I sat back, relaxed, and snapped the occasional photograph. Fleeting attempts at capturing the moments in a bottle, or picture, to relive another time and share with others. Brandon could be seen out in the distance a mile or so out. Ranches were sparsely sprinkled among the landscape as far as you could see any where that was not consumed by the towns borders. As I relaxed I took note that the sun was beginning to relax itself toward the horizon as well. A bright orange orb burning its way through the sky, plummeting toward the horizon, reflecting its glory onto anything around to catch it. The first colors of the painting were just starting to show as they were splashed onto the few clouds that were rolling by. It felt as though I was living in a dream. I felt like I was suspended in the sky as a painter began a masterpiece on a giant canvas in front of me. Sunsets have always mystified me with their beauty as the sky is painted over in all different colors. The significance with the setting of another day has beckoned to me since I was young. Thought of who the sun might be rising on as I sit there and watch it go over the horizon have always drawn me in. My mind drifts to those that are about to wake up and continue the wave of life as it moves around the marble. It is like the breath, coming and going without thought unless we pause and escape the chaos and bask in the moment to watch as it moves through the body.

The colors of the painting were just being washed across the sky - blending together like water colors. The master painter was bringing together hues of orange, red, pink, and even some purples on the opposing horizon. A few puffy clouds meandered across the canvas enhancing the sight and offering some depth into the frame. I stayed and soaked up the work while I finished my pipe. I had packed my headlamp but did not intend to use it. The smell of hot dogs cooking on an open flame were rushing through my mind, even though the fire had yet to start the spark was alive. The painting was finishing as I meandered my way back down the path home. Theres something about a walk through the forest at dusk that feels magical, like walking through an eerie shadow world, all the animals scurrying around before bed with their various chatter.

There was just enough light left in the day as I got back to camp that I had time to ready my fire and get it started without the need of my headlamp. After getting the fire rolling comfortably I realized I had acquired more wood than I would burn through. I noticed the neighbor family I had briefly greeted earlier was scurrying about camp so I headed over to see if they were interested in my extra firewood. They were more than delighted and thanked me graciously. We got so caught up in introductions and conversation that unbeknownst to me my fire was dwindling out behind my back. I had no concern for these matters at the time, the thought of my fire had completely left my mind as I was basking in the light that was this moment with these lovely souls. They were from Minnesota and headed west for Badlands National Park. I also had plans to go to Badlands on my way to Wyoming and stay for a night at the backcountry site. I told them about my journey toward Wyoming to sit in totality of the eclipse. Upon realizing my love for adventure and seeing new, beautiful things they recommended I check out they north shores of Lake Superior, which has been added to my list. Before heading back to camp to re-stoke my fire, rebuild would be a better term, I offered up supplies for s'mores if they didn't have them and were interested. They had most of the things but I was able to supply some graham crackers that were needed to complete the puzzle. We exchanged hugs, love, appreciation, and thanks before I headed back over to camp to relight my fire and cook dinner.

The fire started just as easy as it had the first time and was rolling again in no time. I slow cooked a couple hot dogs over the fire. I added a couple logs after they were done cooking. It was just crisp enough that sitting a few feet from the fire was comfortable. Watching a fire dance has always drawn my attention to it. The flames flashing in and out of existence in every moment. I often watch my mind dance in the same way with thoughts flashing on and off through it, occasionally eating through me like the flames as they burn through a log. I would occasionally glance up at the patch of clear sky through the trees and gaze at the stars but would mainly concentrate on the fire. A few meteors would shoot through the sky dragging tails of various size and grandeur behind them.

As the last of the firewood burned down to ember I embraced the moment to make the perfect s'more and prepped a couple graham crackers with chocolate. I grabbed a couple marshmallows and let them slowly roast over the burning coals, turning them every few seconds. Once they had reached the peak of their possibilities I quickly transferred them to the crackers before they fell from the loving grasp of the twig. I watched the embers flash in and out while I enjoyed my snack, reminiscing of being young and enjoying s'mores around a fire. After about a half an hour I grabbed some water and doused the hot coals, ensuring that there would be no instances of any sparks around to jump. Once I was assured I had it well enough out I headed to my tent.

I would read a couple dozen pages or so before opening up my atlas to get ideas for the next leg of my adventure. There was not much decision to be made as I had already planned to stop at Badlands tomorrow but looked to see if anything attracted me before reaching it to check out - it offered another rather short day behind the wheel. I closed the map and picked up my book to finish reading. I was reading a book by Ram Dass called Be Love Now. I had been turned on to him through my exploration into weird documentaries and movies. He is a spiritual figure who began teaching what he had learned in the 1970's and 1980's. Although I have never met him his voice speaks to me and his messages resonate within me. He has certainly been a spiritual teacher I have followed - a guiding light. He offers a Western perspective on Eastern ideology. I had hardly finished the chapter before my eyes began traversing the gate between this realm and the dream realm.

The purpose of this life is to grow your heart. To learn to love more freely, unconditionally, and unending - in every moment.

CHAPTER FOUR

Good Times in The Badlands

Day Three: 08/18/2017

After a restful night of sleep I woke up and emerged from my tent before the sun rose. As I made coffee and breakfast I noted the dew on my rainfly glistened like stars twinkling in a clear sky at night when the beam from my headlamp radiated it. I calculated I would have roughly an hour or two for the sun to get high enough in the sky to lift the shade of the trees from my tent and dry it off. I decided to go for a hike and soak in some of the morning rays of sun and come back and pack my (hopefully dry) tent. I packed a couple snacks and some water into my daypack and headed out.

I decided to take the path that ran around the perimeter of the park. The birds were busy singing their praise, just as joyous about the beautiful weather as I was. It felt as though they were singing to the sun - calling it out of hiding over the horizon. The first signs of day were beginning to show as the sun slowly worked its way toward the horizon. The eastern horizon burned with light from the sun near its edge, like the light under a doorway in a dark hallway. I passed a few rabbits and squirrels just starting to scurry through the forest and meadows. A couple turtles had already found a spot along the banks that would be in the suns glow in less than an hour. A majority of the forest creatures, including people, were still snuggled in their beds. Other than a few joggers the birds, squirrels, rabbits, and turtles were my only companions along my hike.

Along the river I found a bench sitting about fifty feet off the trail overlooking the river with a perfect view of the sunrise as sun peeked over the horizon. The first strokes of color began to be placed upon the canvas. I took advantage of the privacy and the moment and packed a small pipe while I enjoyed the painting unfold. I had a cardinal singing to me from a branch about ten feet away, glowing a bright red in the fresh rays of sunshine. I have heard that when a cardinal comes and visits you it is the soul of a loved one who passed away - I'm always pulled to memories of my grandmother and the magical moments we shared as she was crossing the path to the next realm. I had the feeling my grandmother was sitting on the bench with me enjoying the painting taking place in the sky. I sang back and forth with the cardinal for a few moments before he flew up and perched on a branch about three feet in front of me. We sat there and shared the view of the beautiful sunrise painting together before we both broke song and went our separate ways. I was back on my way just as the sun was getting high enough in the sky to start burning off some of the colors from the sky.

Meandering slowly back toward camp I kept having this overwhelming feeling that my grandmother was right there walking with me, still holding my hand. Thoughts of her rushed through my mind. I walked slowly, enjoying the moment of sharing a stroll with my grandmother again. I felt her presence with each step. Every bird that sang seemed to carry her voice with it - constant reminders of her love for music. Every flower carried her essence and reminded me of her love for flowers. Rounding a corner a cardinal streaked across my path and into the trees off to the right when a lilac bush caught my eye. Normally I would not recognize a lilac bush this time of year, especially from the distance it was at, except that a single branch had a bloom of lilac flowers which is odd since they bloom in spring and I was hiking in August. It was just another sign of my grandmother's presence as she always loved lilacs.

Arriving back to camp I was pleased to find my tent was now sitting in full sun light. Most of the dew had been evaporated off by the morning sun. My neighbors from Minnesota were also sitting out in the sun enjoying the warming rays while reading. As I passed by I tried to offer a brief "Hello" to avoid interrupting their reading but they did not seem to mind as they put their books down to pick up conversation. They asked about the morning hike and we chatted about plans for the day and life. I explained the idea of going on the hike to give my tent time to dry. From the looks of things they had roughly another hour before their sun broke the shade to dry their tent off. We left each other with love and thanks as I headed back to pack

The Long Road Home

up my sleeping gear and break down camp and leave them to their books again.

After everything was broken down and packed back into the appropriate sacks I began to reload them into the car when something caught my eye as it glistened in the morning sun. I had brought along some necklaces I had made to gift along the way and this seemed to be the perfect place to start. I wrap rocks I've found along my various adventures to make necklaces and the sun was reflecting off some of the wire holding one of the rocks. I grabbed them and headed over to the neighbors camp as they were breaking down their own encampment preparing to head out as well. I offered them each one to which they all graciously accepted. I packed the last couple items into my car and waved goodbye as I headed down the road back out of the park. I took a thirty minute trip southwest to Sioux Falls South Dakota, to stop at a bank before heading off to Badlands National Park.

The trip to the bank went by fairly smoothly with traffic light and flowing. Even with minimal traffic it was still odd to be in the confines of a fairly large city again. After stopping at the bank I got some gas and got back onto the interstate to head back to I-90 west toward the Badlands. Once I was headed west again the landscape was filled with different herds of cattle spread out grazing on the beautiful green grass on the prairies. My mind drifted between the beauty I was experiencing, the beauty I had experienced, and the beauty I had yet to experience.

What felt like a few miles later but may have been a hundred miles or so the scenery shifted to rolling hills. I would cross the Mighty Missouri River after a few more miles. As I approached the river it's grandeur left me speechless. It never gets much mention next to the other rivers that have chiseled the land. The Mississippi seems to get all the attention as it cuts America apart from end to end or the Colorado as it carves a path through Arizona as deep as The Grand Canyon. My mind was pulled toward the unrest at Standing Rock Indian Reservation as the Dakota Access Pipeline was set to run through their land (without their permission) and the potential to damage their only water source - the one I was currently crossing- The Missouri River. I took a moment to consciously meditate on peace, love, and strength for my native kin. I have always felt a pull of peace toward Native Americans and their ideals of living as one with nature. My heart aches when I think of the atrocities caused to them when the early pioneers "settled" their land (gosh, that term sure seems gentle, doesn't it). I try to live in connection to the earth as the natives had, though I know most times I am far off. I thought about stopping at Standing Rock to offer my love and peace to them but I figured with everything going on there it was best to wait.

On the western side of the Missouri River the plains continued to be broken up by rolling hills as I rolled down the road. I was moving along at a good pace, in light traffic, enjoying the scenery and the cool breeze whirling through the open windows. About an hour later I caught sight of some interesting light colored rocks jutting out along the distant horizon, it had to be The Badlands. The closer I got the more certain I became that I was almost to the Badlands. Even at a distance I could feel the magic.

As I came down the road into The Badlands my breath was taken away by the beauty - I was in awe. I tried to imagine how it was formed. I imagined it initially being pushed out of the ground and then weathered by nature, slowly, over time. Even partially comprehending how it was formed I was still complexed by it's brilliance and beauty. It pokes through the plains and rolling hills like nothing from around there. White towers (spires) jolting out of the lush green of the prairies and rolling hills reaching for the sky. It seems out of place, but in the right place at the same time.

I passed through the park gates and continued on the only road leading through the park. Off to the left there was a parking lot for a few different trail heads (where hiking trails start) that was halfway filled with cars. Prioritizing getting camp established -I had no intentions on hiking today. The primitive sites fill up by late afternoon on most days and I wanted to definitely get a spot. I went past the Welcome Center/Gift Shop, I would be back tomorrow, and meandered down the only road that carves through the park. I was going as slow as possible taking in all the sights pulling off to the side, when possible, to let any cars caught behind me get by. Aside from these stops I only stopped a few times to take advantage of opportunities for pictures that were too good to pass up. I followed the winding road through the park admiring the spires and ridges that rolled in waves across the landscape. Each painted in layers of whites, pink and red hues, and even some oranges. Occasionally there would be a break in the rock formations filled with long prairie grass. A few of the rocks had a group of people taking in the scenery or getting ready to head off on a hike down the trail that disappeared over the rocks. A few small groups of big horn sheep also dotted the rocks,

The Long Road Home

blazing their own trails. Each twist seemed to offer a new wave of beauty.

Coming around a corner I was not paying much attention to my maps when I came to a dirt road turn-off on the left. I figured this had to the road to camp and took it. After crossing over some cattle grates in the road (metal grates put down over the road to prevent livestock from crossing where a fence isn't feasible.) the road made a couple twist. After a mile or so I came into a tiny town - really a few houses and a bar. Once again I found my self out of place and going into a bar to help gain clarity on my way. Sure, a bar isn't somewhere you would usually think to go to gain clarity but here I was.

After sharing a few laughs and smiles with my comrades in the bar I found out I had turned too soon, I needed to head back to the main road and go over The Pinnacles and my road would be after that on the left. I headed back toward the main road. When I got to The Pinnacles I took advantage of the solitude and scenery and headed down the quarter mile or so path to the overlook. The pinnacles is the highest point along the road in the park and the view over the park is magnificent. I sat down on the bench and enjoyed a bowl of snacks while I peered out at the scenery. The spires and ridges seemed to roll off in waves disappearing into the horizon, everything seemed like magic and I felt as though I was in deep connection with the source of the magic - in a dance. After finishing my bowl of snacks and spending a little bit of time meditating I headed back down the path toward my car. Just as I was getting in another couple was pulling up and it felt all the more perfect that we'd each get to enjoy the moment in peace.

Before too many more curves in the road I was turning down my road to camp. It was a dirt road, barely two lanes, that was washboard for roughly two-thirds of the time. I couldn't decide if it was a smoother ride to go slightly faster or slightly slower so I spent my time alternating between the two. Perhaps I had hopes of reaching clarity in the matter but really I just alternated each time I got frustrated with the ride the other had offered. A mile or two down the road and I had reached camp, the main loop was full of campers but I was able to find a spot off toward the back where there was a little more space if anyone was daring enough to pull a camper back here. I found my spot and got to setting up my tent and sleeping gear. I had read that bison frequently passed through camp in the evening and/or morning as they roamed the park. I sat under the shade of the tailgate on my

CR-V while I ate some lunch and relaxed. I noticed the hill behind camp had some trails meandering up it from various points and decided it looked like something fun to explore. I loaded up my daypack with snacks and drinks while I relaxed, making sure to include my camp chair. The comfort it offers is always worth lugging it along. Plus it's only one pound and roughly the size of a loaf of bread so it doesn't require much space.

I finished the chapter I had started in my book and tucked the bookmark back into it's space and set my book into the car in exchange for my daypack and walking stick. I headed up the hill carefully selecting the route that took me the most scenic route to the highest point. Not many people were on the hill in front of me or coming up behind me. I found a bank of trees that was almost at the peak and decided this would be a good spot to peek around before turning back. At the top I noticed a couple of hikers across the valley on the next ridge over. I wondered which trail took them there but was not interested enough to venture out to find it. I took in a few deep breaths, solidifying my connection and headed back down the hill to find a spot to enjoy the views with some snacks. I found the perfect rock, flat and maybe ten feet in diameter and I set up my camp chair, took out a couple snacks, and packed a pipe to enjoy with the views. While sitting there clearing my mind I heard some commotion coming down the hill and turned to notice the couple on the ridge across the valley were coming down. It turns out I was on the trail that led over there. It had only been maybe a half hour since I spotted them so it couldn't of been a long hike either. They were a lovely young couple maybe in their mid to late twenties from Missouri. They stopped and chatted for a bit. Sensing a shared love (either from my hair, my aura, or my pet skunk hidden in my pocket) they asked if I wanted to share a pipe of cannabis with them. I obliged and packed a fresh pipe of my own to offer in the sharing. Who was I to turn down such a generous offer?

We sat around for some time chatting about life and sharing stories of our adventures before deciding to head down to camp to get dinner. As we traversed the trail back down toward camp I was in the middle of telling a story when we came around a bend in the trail and stumbled by a gentleman, maybe in his thirty's, sitting down enjoying the view in solitude. Before we came rumbling down the hill with my deep, carrying voice leading the way. I apologized upon seeing him for my loud voice joking that my friends always give me a hard time

The Long Road Home

about whispering. He looked back at me with the most pure and loving smile and I could feel his love radiating through me. He told me he did not mind my voice coming down the hill, he loved it. I could feel the sincerity in his kindness. My heart swelled and I beamed back at him with loving appreciation and gratitude and wished him love and peace. When I left on this trip I made sure it was an adventure with the conscious intention of spreading my light while finding the light of The Universe. Maybe I could find where they converge. Each turn in the path has left me with the feeling that this has all been created and curated for me - even like I've been co-creating it all. I was floating in a pool love with the souls I was surrounded by now, out of mere happenstance. I've never been one to believe much in coincidences or accidents though. Rather I have always seen a connection and synchronicity in the bubbles that pop around me. This kind soul had just reassured me, with love and grace, the value, beauty, and power in my voice and my self. I was left stumbling down the hill in loving awe.

I've found that the more you can open your heart and shower the world with love, appreciation, and gratitude the more the world will continue to shower these things on you in various form. The key is to live with no expectations of what may come or how it comes about, just love and let it be. Have a vision of the beauty you would like to create while remaining open to how it may be brought about.

After a couple turns in the path I looked up and noticed the sun was just getting ready to set, more than likely what the kind gentleman was getting ready to enjoy as we stumbled by and broke his solitude, which he accepted with grace and love. I parted ways with my Missouri friends as I found a beautiful spot to sit and enjoy the sunset. I have never been one to turn down the opportunity to watch a masterpiece as it's created on the great canvas in the sky. I took my chair back out of my backpack and sat back to relax and enjoy the moment with the added benefit of a half packed pipe to finish from earlier. The sun was just beginning to settle over the hills in the distant horizon and the sky was just being painted with hues of pinks, reds, and violets. A few puffy clouds dotted the sky adding another layer of depth. There was a sole pine tree about 15 feet away, that was bing silhouetted, that made the whole thing look like something you might see hanging on a wall somewhere to be admired by whoever might pass and enjoy it. Here it was hanging on the wall of The Universe, as it was being created, for me to enjoy as I passed by. I was filled with peace and joy at the chance I noticed the artist preparing the canvas for the painting before I got down to camp.

When the last colors were being set to dry and dissipate into the dark stillness of the night I packed up my camp chair to head down for dinner. Peering over the horizon in the final, subdued beams of light still filling the air I noticed some bison moving toward camp in the distance. It looked like they would be passing by and missing camp but I went down hopeful I might see one before I let my self roam the land of dreams. As I made my way down to camp I decided on a backpacker meal for dinner as it would be easiest to prep and clean up while offering a satisfying and filling meal.

While waiting for my food to rehydrate I restocked my daypack with a couple snacks and drinks and swapped out my chair for a light blanket and jacket to lay out and look at the stars. The sky was crisp and clear and would be perfect for star gazing. I picked a surprising good beef stew meal That I enjoyed while I sat back and read while relaxing and enjoying the moment. I was in no rush to finish and get moving as I had roughly an hour or so until I would start to have optimal star gazing opportunities. When my stew was finished and I had surpassed a couple chapters through my book I cleaned up and put on some pants and a lightweight long sleeve shirt to ward off any potential mosquitos. I made sure my headlamp was in my daypack. Just before I headed back up the hill toward my destination for star gazing one last visitor pulled up to set up camp, while at near capacity they were able to nestle themselves back with us stragglers. As pulled in I noticed how quiet it was, even with a full campground.

I was headed out to gaze as they were getting out to stay. When I got up the trail to a flat spot I had scoped out on my earlier excursion up the hill. I had used the pine tree near where I had watched the sunset as a marker. I laid out my blanket and got comfortable laying down. Offering just enough plush comfort I decided to use my jacket as a pillow. The stars have always seemed to allow me to navigate my way, through my thoughts and the chaos of life, back to the calm center where my light resides. I've never known if its that looking up at all the beauty makes me feel minuscule in the mix of things or if its that the array of lights, flashes, and flickers makes me feel like I'm looking at a reflection of the depths of my own mind. Either way they have always brought a great sense of peace and connection. The sky was beautiful and clear, there were more stars than I have ever seen - the Milky Way was so bright it seemed to cast a shadow - I was blessed to witness a few shooting stars dash across the sky in whatever way they decided to burn up. I noticed my eyes were getting heavy and I almost dozed off looking at the stars. I decided after one last shooting star to offer thanks and appreciation to The Universe and head back down to camp to get into my comfortable bed.

I got into my tent with just enough energy to read one chapter of my book after I looked at the map in hopes of finding somewhere that drew my attention. I only planned to stay the one night in the park and was getting up early to break down my tent and head back down the main road, the way I came in. I had two hikes planned before taking off down the road; the Door Trail and the Notch Trail. I settled on heading toward Big Horn National Forest the next day as it offered a near mid point between here and Dubois where I was meeting the rest of the guys on the side of the mountain for our hike up the mountain to watch the Total Eclipse in totality. I put my map and book aside with just enough energy to reach up and turn the lantern off before heading off to the realm of dreams.

The minuscule things reverberate out and become the monumental things.

CHAPTER FIVE

Badlands, Black Hills, and Big Horn

Day Four: 08/19/2017

When I opened my eyes I was instantly filled with excitement. I realized I only had two more days until the eclipse. I would adventure around today and find a spot to camp. Tomorrow I would make my way to Dubois Wyoming to meet up with my friends on the side of the mountain. We'd make the mile or two hike up the mountain to camp. The following day we would be basking in the Totality of a Total Solar Eclipse, in solitude. A once in a lifetime experience. I kicked whatever covers remained on me into the darkness of the tent with this joy. I poked my head out of the tent to find the sun tucked behind the horizon still. The first signs of morning still hidden in the faint light as it breaks through the darkness before dawn. Peering toward the horizon I had enough time to get some breakfast and coffee before heading up the hill to watch the sunrise. I ate a bowl of cereal while I waited for my coffee to percolate on my backpacking stove and filled my water bottle up before stashing it in my daypack, along with my camp chair and some snacks. I finished my cereal and did a quick backcountry wash, swirled a little water around in my bowl and wiped it out with my towel. I grabbed my pack and was off to watch the sunrise.

I set up my camp chair and sat back and relaxed, looking up the sky was darker the further west you looked and the last couple stars still dotted the skies where the darkness allowed it. Sitting here I felt like I was on top of the world getting ready to watch a master artist begin a masterpiece right before me. A couple clouds dotted an otherwise clear canvas. The sun was just beginning to stick his crown up above

The Long Road Home

the horizon, the light burned through the darkness and vanished it before you could realize. That's the way life is though, isn't it? If we can just hold our light when faced with darkness then the darkness has no choice but to flee. Reminds me of an analogy I heard watching one of the weird documentaries I watch: You can go into the darkest room - full of the most hatred, anger, and fear - with the tiniest candle and instantly the darkness flees. But you can never do the opposite. You can never go into a well lit room - full of love, appreciation, and gratitude - with any amount of darkness and have any effect.

The scenery was beautiful as the darkness was cast out by the light. The sun kissed off the spires, ridges, and hills and enhanced the colors they already held. The sky was on fire with hues of reds and oranges. Out in the distance some bison were meandering across the prairie headed in the direction of camp. At camp people were starting to shuffle around and go about getting ready for whatever activities they had planned for the day. I sat back and took in a few deep breaths to center my self in the moment, as I was full of enjoyment and awe in it.

Once the sun was about half way over the horizon it had burned off most of the colors it had just splashed across the sky. I sat a few more moments and enjoyed it before packing my chair to head down to camp. I came down the trail and was coming around my neighbors truck to break down my tent and head out. As I turned the corner I was frozen in my tracks by a bison scratching his back on a post used to tie up horses, maybe 15 feet in front of me. I slowly backed away to give some distance between the two of us and give my self options to duck out if needed. I slowly pulled my phone out and snapped a couple photos while I enjoyed the majestic presence before me. After maybe ten or fifteen minutes of scratching he meandered off down the way. I let him gain a little distance before going to break down my tent. I had everything broken down and packed back in the car within a half hour. I was back in the car heading out..

I had the same constant debate of faster or slower over the washboard road leading back to the main road. I turned right onto the main road and headed back the way I came in yesterday. I drove just as slow since I was seeing everything in a whole new light, from a new perspective. Some prairie dogs were out enjoying the early morning sun - a few stood on guard watching the horizon. I did not have to pull off to the side to let many cars by as the road was still fairly tame with most folks just getting their day started. I passed by the gift shop as I wanted to hit the two trails I had planned before too many people got out. The weather was beautiful and I imagined it wouldn't be too long before they started to descend.

    I decided on heading down the notch trail first. Both trail heads were in the same parking lot, the door was slightly closer to the gift shop where I was working my way back toward before finally leaving the park. I put some snacks and drinks in my pack and put my hiking boots on to head down the trail. It starts off weaving its way between rock cliffs and outcroppings taking you deeper into a canyon. After about twenty minutes of meandering down the trail I came across a couple in their sixties. I was immediately impressed they were out here as the trail I had done so far had a couple small climbs and scrabbles to get up rock levels. I offered them a joyous and loving hello as they reciprocated it back toward me. When I learned their age upon curiously asking I praised them with hopes that I would still be crushing trails out at their age. Before parting they told me I was just about to a ladder that took you up onto the ridge top. I forgot my buddy Andrew had told me about this ladder. A few more turns in the trail and I came to the ladder, a rope ladder with wood steps that goes up maybe a twenty-five to fifty feet, an interesting turn in an already beautiful trail. After the ladder you weave your way across the ridge following a designated trail, marked with post at critical points, as their are cliffs and drop-offs all around. A quarter mile of following this trail and you are led to a look out - a notch in the rocks - overlooking the park. I made my way up and sat in the notch and enjoyed some snacks and a few puffs from my pipe as I soaked in the moment and snapped a couple pictures. I headed back down the trail. Just as I got to the section were you follow the ridge a family of four was making their way up to the notch. I've been baffled by the amount of times I have been offered just the perfect timing of things like solitude to enjoy a view or moment. When I got to the ladder their was a family of maybe ten who ranged in age from about six to sixty working their way down the ladder. They had roughly half up and half down and offered me to go ahead but I passed up the offer taking advantage of the small little break and chance to enjoy this moment. The trip down the ladder was certainly a little trickier to navigate at first than the way up and I wondered if facing toward the ladder or away would be easier to get down. I only spent a moment debating and ended up facing out and got down fine. The family was down at the bottom of the ladder getting organized for the hike out and I wished them happiness and love before heading out. After a bend or two in the trail a beautiful red tail hawk soared above. I paused a moment to enjoy his presence and imagined the view offered from soaring so freely above this plane.

About a quarter mile or so before the parking lot I caught up with the couple I had met on the way up. Just starting their hike again after stopping in the shade for a break and snacks. They offered me to pass but I suggested meandering with them as I was in no hurry and wouldn't mind the company as long as they didn't. We handled formal introductions, Bill and Rita were out enjoying retirement. They were also on a journey to catch the eclipse. They lived in Kansas but were out enjoying the country for a month or two. I praised them again for being out crushing out hikes still while enjoying life. I joked, only partially, that I was trying to live the retired life now in a constant effort and process to balance work time with time for my self and adventure. We talked about life and philosophies and I told them my goals to reach Wyoming to catch the eclipse on a journey to spread my love and joy along the way. The idea made them happy and they instantly lit up with smiles that radiated. All three of their adult children and four grand children live fairly close to them. I took advantage of the opportunity to brag about my daughter and our shared love for adventure. When we reached the end of the trail we snapped a few pictures together before exchanging hugs, love, peace, and goodbyes.

When we parted ways I headed down the parking lot toward the door trail. The trail started as a boardwalk that traced along side a rock wall for a few hundred feet before curving around an opening in the rock. Immediately after the bend it opened up and there was a deck with a bench for sitting to the left and stairs sat directly in front as you. They led down to follow post along the ridge top. I went down the stairs and followed the trail as it bent around the rock wall the boardwalk followed. Right as I turned the corner I was once again stopped in my tracks staring down a beast ten feet away. This time a couple big horn sheep who were walking back toward were I was coming from stood right where I wanted to go. I slowly walked away backwards, facing them the entire time and talking in a calming manner to them. They followed back with each step I took, never in a threatening manner but rather happy I was getting out of their way. I went back up the stairs and stood on the deck. They passed on by appearing to follow the trail to the parking lot. Once the coast was clear and they had passed by I went back down the stairs and carefully poked around the rock wall - everything was clear. The trail followed on top of a ridge that had washed out canyons. After about 200 feet there were numbered post you followed to avoid any of the rather dangerous canyons. When I got to the end of the trail, a giant tabletop rock with a nice view waited for me, there was a family there enjoying the moment as well. We offered to snap pictures for each other and briefly exchanged greetings before they headed back down the trail.

    Glancing back toward where the trail began I noticed there was nobody coming that I could see - figuring I might be offered thirty minutes to enjoy the view to my self - I sat down to relax in the moment.   As I took a few deep breaths in I closed my eyes and listened to all the sounds around me. Birds chirped while they rushed to and from their homes nestled in the rock ledges and the wind swirled around the spires and cliffs. Just as I opened my eyes a beautiful red tail hawk was soaring above, perhaps the same one I had seen on the previous trail. Seeing the hawk soar brought a feeling of connection to Source that I have felt all along this journey following my heart. It felt as though I had spread my wings to catch the drafts of air from The Universe (the flow) and was soaring. I took a few puffs from my pipe as I relished in the connectedness before getting up to head back down the trail and on my journey. Just as I was leaving another group was coming up to enjoy the outlook, perfectly timed again. I was leaving as my solitude was coming to an end. I worked my way back down the trail following the numbered post.

    Coming off the boardwalk onto pavement I noticed a bench about twenty feet away and stopped by for a short break, not needed but desired, to take in everything around me. The parking lot was filling up quickly as groups of people were out enjoying the weather and the park. I took the time to close my eyes and take a few more deep breaths. I watched them move through my body as the noise from the crowds in the parking lot swirled around me. My soul was being re-energized as the morning sun kissed me with a warm glow. I looked around at the landscape I would be leaving sooner than I would like. My senses were being played like the keys on a piano by a great composer - in harmony and timing as the masterpiece unfolded. A sense of harmony took me over as I sat there. I headed to my car to start my next leg of my journey when I felt pulled to. The next leg would take me to meeting up with my buddies on the side of a mountain.

    After a quick stop by the gift shop for souvenirs for my daughter I

The Long Road Home

stopped by the gas station for fuel, coffee, and snacks. I was headed back west down the highway. After an hour or so I came into the Black Hills National Forest boundary and shortly after passed a sign for the Spearfish Canyon Scenic Route - again the signs from The Universe pulled me where needed. I followed the detour as it vanished into the forest. The route traversed the forest, crossing streams and small towns, and cutting through the canyon. There were plenty of opportunities to stop for pictures or whatever along the way. I took advantage of as many as possible for pictures and found the perfect spot for lunch. It was nestled right by a stream with a trail that followed the water back into the woods. After eating I took a small hike back through the woods to take some time with nature. Wildflowers were in bloom in various shades, bundled like a bouquet to be enjoyed, all around. The birds were singing their praise as butterflies danced about between the flowers. The wind carried the sweet fragrance of the wildflowers past me and ticked my noise with their radiance. After roughly a quarter mile I found a nice pool in the stream to sit near. I went and sat by the waters edge to listen to it move as I puffed on my pipe. There was a certain harmony the way the birds were singing as the water moved over the rocks with a humble ripple and the flowers reflecting off the pool of water - their reflections dancing with every ripple in the water. After treasuring this moment for thirty minutes or so I headed back down the trail towards my car. On the way back down the trail I noticed a few trout in the water. I had not seen any on the way in. When they caught sight of me they would dash behind a rock to hide, blending in like they were never there. I got back to my car and refilled my cup with some tea before heading back down the road. After an hour or so more of slow driving through the beautiful scenes I was about to meet up with the highway. I stopped for some gas before heading down the interstate at a less leisurely pace.

After a few hours of my mind moseying with my car down the road I took my exit that would take me to Big Horn National Forest where I would camp for the night. Unsure of where I would camp I just drove around and enjoyed the views until I felt pulled to stop somewhere. Generally one of the benefits of camping in a national forest is the benefit of camping for free but I ended up finding the perfect spot that cost me less than twenty dollars with a bundle of wood included - free enough for me. A campground right by a small lake called the Sibley Lake Campground caught my attention and I pulled in. I found the

35

perfect spot with a picnic table, room to hang my hammock, cook dinner, and relax.

I set up my hammock and built a fire just small enough to cook a couple hot dogs for dinner and not too much longer. I wanted to go out and take a small hike after dinner and didn't want to spend too much time around a campfire for now. I boiled some water while the dogs cooked to make some instant mashed potatoes. I alway prefer the real thing over instant but these taste remarkably good and in the situation there really was no choice. After eating the dogs and half the mashed potatoes, deciding to save the rest as a snack later, I cleaned up and packed my daypack with some necessities. Once I had a couple snacks and drinks loaded in my daypack I headed off on a trail just below camp I had noticed when setting up that appeared to lead around the lake. It weaved it's way through the pine forest and gave a nice view of the lake below between the trees before it left my view. Birds sang their songs all throughout the trees. I spotted a couple of woodpeckers searching for food as the repetitive tap echoed through the forest. I hiked on for roughly an hour before finding a good spot to relax and turn back. On the way back to camp I noticed a perfect place to watch the sunset across the lake. It was only about a twenty minute hike from camp. Looking at the distance from the horizon to the sun I sensed that I had roughly one and a half hours before sunset. I never move too fast or worry about distance traversed on these hikes, something I constantly work towards implementing on the journey of life as well, as I focus more on just enjoying the beauty and magic offered in each moment. Something I've found in life is that most of my mistakes have been made in moments when I get in a rush.

Back at camp I grabbed a couple handfuls of trail mix, moved my chair into the sun light, and sat down to soak in the light. I closed my eyes and opened my heart to soak in this moment and everything that has led to it. Taking time away from the chaos of daily life to slow down and find peace within while chasing the path of my hearts joy has become a fundamental part of my life. I have always been the kind to move against the grain rather than following societal standards. This has been more amplified the past four or five years since losing my job at Redbox. My decisions have left most everyone around me questioning my reasoning and plans. I realized I would rather work toward the dreams of my heart before working towards a dream that isn't mine and does not radiate with my heart. Doing things that allow me more time to adventure and enjoy life now as opposed to finding a long term career. I don't like conventional wisdom that tells us work now and do the things you really want when you retire. Allotting more time for adventuring out into nature while simultaneously adventuring inward. I have taken the time to do more internal work to find the corners where my shadow hid, to go and sit with it, not to push it away but to welcome it in and see it as a part of my self. It's a constant work toward self love - but when you think about self love you cannot choose to only love the aspects or parts of your self that make you seem more appealing, you must love all parts the same. Realize that even the aspects you see as darkness are all a part of the light that is the being of your soul. The more you know and understand the aspects you don't desire instead of pushing them away like they don't exist the less they will consume you from the depths of your self you've been pushing them to the whole time. They are all aspects of the light that is you, and they radiate together. The more you push things you don't like away the more these things crowd the depths of your self where your light resides. Shading your light and preventing it from radiating its beauty. Fear of the unknown will lock you in a chamber much more confining than any jail cell could ever hope to. Akin to never really living life in fear of death when the greatest death is of a life not lived.

Looking through the trees as I opened my eyes I realized I had roughly a half hour until the suns light was setting. I quickly rolled a small joint to enjoy while the painting unfolded and packed some snacks and water bottles into my daypack along with my chair and headlamp. I grabbed a light jacket and laced my boots up and headed out, in near perfect timing for things to come.

The Universe had gifted me the perfect space to witness the sun setting. Looking out through the pine forest the lake was down below with the sun setting on the opposite side. Off in the distance there were two mountains whose bases met at the horizon and they climbed together in opposite directions. The sun would set near directly in the middle of them. A few clouds dotted the sky and the birds were singing their final songs for the night. A cardinal and I talked as the sun was setting before he parted and flew to another tree in the distance. I could still hear him sing. As the sun nestled into the valley of the mountains on the distant horizon it burned a radiant red. The sky was being painted with radiant hues of pinks and reds. All the beauty in the sky was being reflected perfectly off the stillness of the lake below. I extinguished my joint as the sunlight was being extinguished by the horizon - enjoying the last splashes of color before the darkness of dusk erased them. Off in the east the first stars could be seen poking through the night sky between the trees.

    Waiting patiently for the stars to come out I sat back and enjoyed some trail mix and tea while I peered around at my surroundings in the remaining faint light still left from the western horizon. Lightning bugs, or fireflies, flashed all around. Occasionally one of the trees would flicker full of lights like a Christmas Tree. The sonar chirp of scattered bats could be heard from above as they dashed around consuming bugs like mosquitos and such. I offered my praise and appreciation to them each time I heard one. The western horizon was still glowing from the sun that had tucked itself somewhere over the distant horizon. As you worked your way east across the sky the darkness consumed more of it. The closer to the eastern horizon I looked the more stars I could see. Occasionally I would be blessed enough to catch glimpse of a shooting star as it traced across the night sky. As I gazed around at all the beauty around me the glow on the western horizon had disappeared as the darkness of night won the battle. The scar of the Milky Way stretched across the sky, bright enough to almost reflect off the lake. I stayed long enough to catch a few more shooting stars and enjoy the rest of the joint I had extinguished earlier.

    I got back to camp and started a small fire with the remaining wood to enjoy before bed. Once I had it rolling nicely I sat back and watched it dance. Off behind me I heard something rustle through the woods, the sound of twigs snapping caught my attention. Focusing my headlamp in the direction I could not see anything. I sat on edge for a couple minutes, keeping quiet to focus my attention toward the woods. I glanced around to make sure I had all food items and smelly items packed away in the car. After a few moments of silence I turned the wood on the fire and went and laid in my hammock to watch the fire dance. I could of easily fallen asleep right there. While I would love to fall asleep to the crackle and warmth of the fire I've never wanted to risk a forest fire. Just as I was relaxing I heard another noise in the woods that quickly slapped me out of any snooze I may have been drifting toward. This time I just sat back and listened, I didn't bother getting a headlamp as I usually don't see a thing. After a few moments I was back in the complete silence of the woods aside from the occasional crack of the fire. Once it burned through the wood and was just hot embers I got out of my hammock and doused the embers with some water to put out the remaining coals. And with the hiss of the water hitting the heat my final vestiges of light were put out. I retreated to my hammock one final time after watering some flowers nearby. It was a perfect night for sleeping, beautifully clear and cool. The chirps and songs of the crickets and night creatures lulled me to sleep before I realized it.

Your wings are hidden in your love. If you want to fly just spread your love and soar.

CHAPTER SIX

Mingling Madness on the Mountain

Day Five: 08/20/2017

Opening my eyes and gazing under my tarp the sky was still dark and everything around me was asleep. In opposition to last night the eastern horizon was now glowing in preparation to welcome the morning sun. I unzipped my bug net and slid out into the darkness to find some flowers in need of water. I decided I would pack up camp, as quiet as possible, and head off on the road. I figured I could find a good spot to catch the sunrise while I ate breakfast and had coffee. The morning birds were just coming out and singing their praise for the day as I took down my hammock and packed it up. The excitement of the day had me awake and refreshed after only four or five hours of sleep. I was bubbling with joy that I would find Dubois today and the familiarity of friends.

   I loaded everything in the car and closed the doors as quietly as possible. I only used my parking lights to illuminate my way through camp to avoid my headlights shining in tents. I headed down the road that winds through the park, with my headlights on. As the horizon began glowing more ferociously the forest was filled with a odd glow that brought about a mysterious feeling. Made it seem like something good was brewing in the cauldron of the day. I came around a bend in the road and the forest opened up to a valley with a meadow stretching over it. I noticed my stomach was becoming more aggravated that I hadn't given it nourishment and love yet. Just then I noticed a small road that almost looked like a driveway converging with the road in about three hundred feet or so. I felt pulled to the spot and it seemed the perfect space with an open view of the eastern

The Long Road Home

horizon to view the sunrise. Pulling in I noticed a sign just ahead, like the address sign hanging on mailbox post in the country that are green with white numbers. This one had the numbers nine, six, three printed in white numbers, vertically, on a brown sign hanging on a wooden post. Here were the three numbers The Universe seems to beckon to me with hanging on a sign directly in front of me. The Universe again pulled me directly where I needed. I've noticed as I have opened my heart more, and followed the path through the gates, my connection with The Universe has become clearer. It's made reacting the flow and going with it easier simultaneously.

We're taught to set goals in life and always push on toward them. That is what generally defines our success. Subsequently our happiness is said to be found through this. One thing I have found as I have moved along this path in life is that as you let go of desires and expectations it opens the space you are in for more unexpected beauty and gifts from The Universe. It grants the chance to be blessed with gifts in ways more splendid than you could imagine. I have been working toward shifting my goals into conscious intentions. Let go and stop pushing for what you desire. Allow The Universe to pull you toward where you're needed instead of pushing against it to get what you desire. Generally speaking the final destination is the same but the trip there will be more enjoyable with less energy wasted. It is a constant practice of letting go of the control you thought you had but never fully grasped. A shift is required to realize that you are a co-creator in this masterpiece of life. As a co-creator it should also be realized that we are creators - with the power to create heaven and hell here and now. Heaven is found when we open our heart and move through love. Hell can be found when we get bound by fear in the webs of our mind. Fear will close the gates to both domains. Love will break them open and allow them to flow.

I unfolded my chair and got a bowl of cereal while my coffee percolated. I was relaxing with a cup of coffee just as the masterpiece was beginning to unfold on the horizon. I had a beautiful foreground as a gentle breeze rushed through the meadow and pushed over the tall grass that lined it. Birds dashed through my scope of view off to start their daily duties. The sky was crisp and clear again with only a few small, puffy clouds dotting it. Off in the distance, on the eastern horizon, two mountains came together and formed a small valley. In the middle of the valley further away was another mountain where the sun was rising directly behind. I was once again caught swirling in the tidal waters of universal flow finding more beauty than anything I could of ever imagined or dreamed. The feeling of everything coming to fruition and blossoming before me. I was going to witness darkness take over the day as two celestial bodies interacted in ways most would never experience first hand. While I was ecstatic to get to Dubois and find friendly faces, the desire to rush down the road was tampered by the thrill of this moment.

I soaked in everything around me as the colors were laid out on the canvas. The ball of fire behind them turned the mountains in the distance a bright red that filled the eastern sky. Hues of orange painted the rest of the sky and clouds.The brilliance seemed to last an eternity but may have only taken thirty minutes. I finished my coffee and poured what was left from the percolator into my travel mug for the ride. I packed up my chair and bowl from cereal and loaded everything into the car. I offered appreciation and gratitude for the moment before getting back behind the wheel and winding down the road through Big Horn National Forest. My path through the forest was filled with opportunities to pull of and enjoy the scenery or hike. Not many would pull me fiercely enough to distract me from the journey to my destination. The pull of Dubois overwhelmed the attraction that most of the forest around me had. Once the road broke out of the serenity of the forest it cut through the Wyoming country side, passing through a few small towns. As I came into the town of Dayton I had to stop for a picture - from Dayton, in Ohio now in Wyoming. This Dayton offered a more quaint, small-town charm. The path leading to Dubois was scattered with people setting up camp in fields and yards. People along the route were offering parking in their yard for a small fee, their frequency increased the closer I got. I couldn't imagine any of them had a space that would hold a candle to the one I was heading to.

Somewhere along the way I lost cell phone reception, I would no longer be able to communicate with my daughter and getting ahold of my buddies to coordinate our rendezvous just got more interesting. I didn't allow any panic to set in about the situation as I was protected from the negativity of that potential by a bubble of joy in the moment.

Dubois was a picturesque western town, it seemed like I was driving through a postcard, wood framed building lined Main Street. Even new buildings like the Dollar General store held the appeal. The old vertical wood plank siding it looked more like a saloon than a dollar store. Coming from the east I was shocked, and in love, with

The Long Road Home

how cut off from the hustle of the outside world and the "comforts" offered by it the west was. Back east their would be a big box store in each of these small towns I had passed but here the small communities, and the people, were more independent. This trip through the west has given me a new respect for the folks out here, especially law enforcement. There is no one around for miles sometimes and the terrain can be unforgiving. You are truly on your own here. A single officer is alone patrolling mass amounts of territory with a majority of the population carrying guns. I imagine back up is not as readily available nearby like it would be back east either. The people are lovely when you come across them, but you may not come cross paths too often. They treat you like a neighbor even though they live in sparse communities with no real neighbors nearby.

I let my mind wander as my GPS directed me down the road. After a few hours I was being directed to turn onto the dirt road to the trail head where me and my buddies were planning to meet. There was a surprising number of people parking here. The trail head offered access to a few trails that cut around the mountains in various directions and totality cut across the mountain. Park rangers were directing people where to park as they pulled in off the main road. The small trail head parking lot was not being used for overnight campers. They were having people who were camping park in fields about a mile or two down the road from the trail head. The gang and I had planned to meet up at the trail head parking lot and while we coordinated via text message and phone throughout the day we obviously hadn't communicated since I lost reception. I listened to where the ranger directed me to park and explained that I was waiting for a buddy and gave him the best description possible of what to look for without knowing what kind of car they rented. It was a shot in the darkest of darks given my description and the fact that this guy was going to be directing hundreds of people. I could imagine he wouldn't think to look for Andrew or recognize him amongst the masses if he did look. I told him I would save him a spot and I intended to.

When I got to the field to park everyone was pulling in and parking nose first, I pulled up sideways to the car I would park by to take up two spaces. I got out to stretch and set my camp chair up in the shade of my tailgate. Before making a sandwich for lunch I took the tarp from my hammock, which was still wet from the morning dew, and laid it over the roof of the CR-V to dry in the wind and sun. More people were filling into the lot as I went over my checklist and gathered things together to put into my backpack. A group pulled up and parked behind me, at what would be the next spot, when they got out I offered a kind hello and quick apology for parking against the grain and offered an explanation. Without asking they generously moved their car over a little more so when Andrew came it would be easier to accommodate moving and parking us both in the space I was saving. They began gathering and sorting their items. Going over their checklist for their trip. Once I was finished organizing I went back to relaxing in my chair which I would just strap to the outside of my pack so it didn't need packed away. As they finished up organizing they were standing around snacking, waiting to get started, when we started discussing our journeys here and plans. I was chatting with the one guy about meeting my buddies here and joked that I might be hiking up the mountain solo if they didn't come. We talked about the excitement that was building up as we got closer to experiencing totality. When I told him I planned on letting out my traditional howl of excitement he asked to hear it. Not holding anything back I let out a howl that echoed through the valley. An echo of howls came back from the various people in the lots. The magic of the movement was reverberating and reflecting through the valley.

Shortly after the howl I was explaining that I was surprised my buddies hadn't pulled in yet. I was just thinking that they may have been directed to another lot when I see a figure walking up over the hill that led to the entrance of the field. Looking closer I noticed it was my buddy Rob and a rush of excitement came over me. We embraced with relief and joy and I told him I was just talking about them. He said they parked over in another lot and he came to to see if he could find me. He said right when he opened the door to get out of the car he heard my howl come from across the way and instantly recognized it as me. The Universe does not mess around when you dance with it in love and joy - it will always find another way to bestow amazement and beauty upon you. Rob made the journey back to retrieve Andrew and Maranda and the car as I beamed with love. I felt like my radiance was matching the sun's brilliance - I was in harmony with the moment. They brought the car over and we exchanged love before they gathered their things while eating some lunch. We didn't waste much time as we wanted to get up and establish camp. We had an additional mile or so of road that we didn't expect to hike before getting to the trail.

We all made sure we had our water bottles and water bladders (bags with a hose for our backpacks) filled to capacity with cold water. I

The Long Road Home

offered everyone an ice cold gatorade and stashed one in my side pocket of my backpack to enjoy down the trail. We headed down the dirt road toward the Glacier Trail Trailhead. A nice breeze pushed across the fields offering some relief from the sun that radiated in the clear sky. It also added to the beauty of the scene as it pushed the tall grasses and flowers over on its way past them. A patch of bright yellow flowers adorned the side of the creek to the left side of the road. We finally made it to the trail and started up the dirt path that traversed over or around the rocks as it ascended the mountain. The trail was fairly baron as we scurried up, we only crossed paths with maybe ten hikers. It was a stark contrast to the parking lot. The hike up wasn't overly strenuous other than the gain in elevation - which we weren't accustomed to. The higher we went the air got thinner and it made it difficult to get adequate oxygen. I didn't have too much of a problem with it but as we got higher the views were taking my breath away and causing me to frequently pause in awe and soak them in. As we were climbing the mountain in front of us most the views were behind us so you basically had to stop to enjoy them. Each stop I would think of my daughter and how I wished she could be here to share this with me. It was driving me mad that I had not talked to her all day. Throughout the trip we talked or text fairly frequently. Our talks daily made it easier to be away from her, that ease quickly slipped away as the day wore on. We passed by a handful of potential spots for camp but passed them with the desire to be higher on the mountain and closer to the alpine lake. We marked them in the memory in case we needed to turn back from lack of opportunity toward the top.

    Once we were roughly a quarter mile from the lake we found the perfect spot for camp right on the river. With enough space for two tents and two perfect trees for me to hang my hammock between. We quickly took our packs off to relax. While surveying the site we decided Andrew and I would head up the mountain to the lake to see if there were any better spots to be had. Maranda and Rob stayed behind to save this spot if not.

    The hike up to the lake was difficult with a steeper climb, even without packs. Once you reached the last climb before the lake it was a tough jaunt up a smooth rock that did not offer much traction and was pitched about fifty degrees or so up, maybe more I forgot my protractor in my backpack. No, I did not pack a protractor. We got to the top and paused for a moment to take in the beauty of the view overlooking the lake. The source of water feeding the lake was about halfway up the mountain behind the lake - a huge glacier appearing to glow in the light of day against the dark colored mountains. Working our way across the ridge and down the cliffs to the various levels of rock that led closer to the waters edge. The lake was a crisp, beautiful blue. It was tucked in between two mountain peaks and fed by glacier melt. The river running by camp was the overflow of the lake. A stiff wind pushing across the top broke the stillness into choppy waves. There was a giant rock jutting out in the middle from the other edge, a peninsula. A well established camp with 3 or 4 tents was nicely situated on it. A gentle white smoke rolled above the pine trees partially lining it. Andrew and I wondered how exactly they got there. The mountain on the edge of the lake the rock met was steep and rugged. Other than that camp there weren't many spots we wanted to camp. Most of them you would be on hard rock with a brisk wind the entire time. Most of the people camped up here were tucked behind rocks when they were hanging out. We quickly realized our spot was superior to anything offered up here. We enjoyed the views for a moment while taking a few puffs from the pipe I had in my pocket before heading back down to set up camp.

   At camp I hung my hammock and tarp while they decided on what was the best configuration of the two tents. As they finished setting up their tents I went about rolling a nice joint to celebrate everything once they were set up. Before smoking the joint we decided to gather firewood so we didn't have to search in the dark. With an adequate stack sitting near our fire ring we sat down to relax for a bit. As the celebratory doob was being lit we admired the beauty around us. There was a raging creek right beside us with plenty of rocks jutting out from the edge that allowed you to go sit on and feel like you were in the middle of the water. A couple trees near the water were spaced just right for the other hammock. It offered somewhere to rest and relax by the water with a view down the mountain as the water carved it's way down into the valley. Across the valley you could see rolling mountains off in the distance.

   When the joint was finished we decided we were getting hungry, surprisingly enough.. Although I argue this was more from the strenuous hike up more than the extracurricular activities we just partook in. Either way our stomachs were talking us in to eating. Andrew and Maranda went about picking what to cook for dinner and Rob and I, who were also sharing meals, got into our food bag to look at our options. Scouring the food the idea to go to the lake after dinner was settled upon. We dug the pots and stoves out of the backpacks and went about boiling water. While we waited for the meals to rehydrate I went out to explore around camp and see what other views were around. After a couple minutes Andrew called me over to camp. They all decided going up to the lake to eat dinner sounded like a better plan as long as I was in, which sounded marvelous. We quickly grabbed our water bottles and eating utensils before grabbing our piping hot dinners and heading up the mountain.

At the top more camps had popped up on the rocks around the lake. We jockeyed our way around them as we worked our way down closer to the edge of the water. We found a nice spot nestled into some rocks, protected from the wind, with some rocks on the waters edge to sit. After three trout jumped out of the water, about ten feet from the shore, all Andrew could do was shake his head. He left his fishing pole back down at camp. When we finished dinner we cleaned up and headed back to camp. We decided while eating dinner that we would head back up for the sunset in about a hour.

Back at camp Andrew and Maranda, not wanting to hike up and down again, decided not to hike back up to the lake for the sunset. We sat around and built a small fire while we snacked on some beef jerky. Suddenly feelings of missing my daughter and hearing her voice rushed over me. I could not stop the thoughts from crashing over me and washing me with sadness. I headed over toward the waters edge to find a rock to sit on and meditate, to be with my sadness for a moment. I have this feeling that maybe when I am thinking about another soul maybe they're thinking about me too at that moment and together our souls are dancing in another realm. My attention was focused on the rush of the water as it crashed into the rocks and rolled over them. I closed my eyes and took a few deep breaths and gave thanks for everything, especially this adventure and the bond my daughter and I share. Opening my eyes my focus was brought back to the waters wrath as it rush over the edge of the mountain and descended into the valley. Sources of water have always called to me, especially moving water like a river. Maybe it was the way the water weaved its way around obstacles, maybe it was its peaceful song. Either way I've never worried too much as to which it was, I just enjoy being near it. There's a certain calming feeling that goes with the life sustaining nature of water. We are one with the river, ever changing. Like Heraclitus said, " No man ever steps in the same river twice, for it is not the same river and he is not the same man." I headed back to the group with my mind cleared. While I still missed my daughter I was at peace in this moment and knowing I would see her in a few days.

While we smoked a small bowl Rob suggested we take a small joint up to the lake to enjoy while the sunset. He disappeared into his tent, out of the wind, and I headed back over to the fire to finish the pipe with Andrew. Sitting there with Andrew I noticed there was a palpable bubble of energy, teeming with excitement in anticipation for the eclipse tomorrow. None of us knew what to expect to see or feel tomorrow other than it being a once in a lifetime experience. The universal drum beat was reaching a feverish pace, building toward a peak. This whole trip I have felt like I was climbing a metaphorical mountain toward a peak that would come tomorrow in totality. Vibrations of energy reverberated out cracking the cocoon that contained the self. Initially I hid my self within to protect it but eventually to transform it.

Sitting around and basking in the energy that bubbled up in the moment, feeding off it as we shared our stories about the adventure that got us here. They had flown over from Dayton to Denver and stayed a couple days there. They caught a Govt. Mule concert at Red Rocks Amphitheater. They told me all about being able to purchase legal weed in Denver and how strange it was to walk out of a store with a bag of it when back home it's handled clandestinely. The had visited The Elevationist Church in Denver the night before coming up. It's a church in Denver that, in some manner, ties cannabis in with scripture. They took in the sermon before taking the Holy Sacrament. The inside of the church is painted elaborately with geometric designs and other art with vivid colors, judging from the pictures they showed me.

As the sun was getting closer to the horizon Rob and I threw some snacks, water, headlamps, and jackets into our daypacks. I grabbed my hiking stick from the tree I leaned it against earlier. We offered Andrew and Maranda peace and farewell before heading up the trail. On the hike up my mind seemed to drift back and forth with each step between excitement for tomorrow, the trip in general, and the sadness that came with missing my daughter. I had not seen her in almost a week and this was my first full day of not hearing her voice. Seeing my friends familiar faces must have brought back familiar feeling of home. The sadness seemed to accompany these feelings near the membrane of my bubble. I was able to mostly subdue the feelings as we talked and soaked in the beauty around us.

Once we reached the top of the mountain we picked a spot overlooking the lake from atop the rocks. We found a nice ledge to sit on to soak in the painter's masterpiece. As the first colors were laid out I mentioned to Rob how blessed I felt being witness to so many beautiful sunsets and sunrises on this trip. I gazed down toward the lake and noticed the colors were reflecting perfectly off its surface, which was now smooth. Each painting from the previous days flashed through my mind. I was starting to see the world as a reflection of my appreciation and gratitude. It was a giant feedback loop. The bowl that contained the lake and people was filled with peace and calm. The moment felt surreal. It seemed like every one was enjoying the sunset. Every few moments a trout would jump out from the waters depths breaking the stillness that pervaded the water and air. Like the minuscule moments in life the ripples expanded outward growing in magnitude until they finally reached the shore. Just as Rob reached into his pocket and asked if I was ready to smoke the joint a rustle broke the silence behind us. We both jolted our heads and attention in the direction the noise came from. Andrew and Maranda were making their way over the long sloped rock that led to the ledge after deciding it was a worthwhile hike. The timing couldn't of been anymore perfect. Just as Andrew was reaching for the snack-stick Rob just lit a trout jumped out of the water about fifteen feet from the edge. My smile grew from ear to ear as the fish seemed to break my bubble of excitement and I could no longer contain my joy. Just as that bubble burst Andrew let out a "dammit" as he once again left his pole at camp. Laughter overtook us as the bubbles of excitement grew. Two more trout jumped from the water, one after the other, brought up from the bubbles. Or perhaps it was just The Universe laughing with us.

Other than a few wispy clouds the sky was clear, being filled with hues of pink, red, and violet. The sun was working its way behind some mountains off in the distance, the next time around would be a magical one. The lower the sun got the darker the silhouettes got that were overtaking the trees. Everything was being reflected off the surface of the lake like a giant mirror. With the last strokes of paint being laid we decided to begin our descent to camp. On our way down the trail we all realized what tomorrow would bring and joy overtook us. Excitement carried us the rest of the way to camp.

Back at camp we all changed into warmer clothes and rekindled the fire. Andrew and Maranda made some hot cocoa. Rob and I decided to mix coffee with our hot cocoa so I started percolating some coffee. This seemed like the perfect cap to an amazing day. Sipping our drinks we decided to take advantage of the clear skies offered for star gazing. Just on the other side of the trail there were rocks to rest on. The trail sat in an opening a couple hundred feet wide. Mountains on either side and the valley down below. The horizon seemed to stretch into eternity. The Milky Way looked brighter than it had any other night so far. There were more stars than one could manage to count in a lifetime. We all got to see at least one shooting star dash across the brilliant sky before we headed back down to camp to tend to and enjoy the fire.

 We sat around talking and enjoyed the dance of the fire and the mix of its crackle with the rumble of the river for about a half hour before Maranda turned in for bed. We grabbed the last snacks out of the food bag before hanging them up for the night. As we added a couple more pieces of wood to the fire we elected to close the night out with some cannabis snacks. Rob packed up a pipe and we headed down to the waters edge to filter some water. After a couple tokes Andrew retired to the tent as well. I tossed a couple small pieces of wood on the fire to finish the night off with Robs approval. We sat around watching the fire dance as it consumed the wood we just added. We added a little more cannabis to the pipe while we watched the embers flicker in and out around the ring.

 After around an hour of watching the embers dance we were both ready to douse the fire with water and head to bed. Just as the first hiss from the water hitting the hot embers was let out we heard the howls from a pack of coyotes off in the distance. Their howls almost brought a howl out of me but I fought the urge, not wanting to wake others. I decided to save it for tomorrow. Rob couldn't hold back his laughter when I told him how close I was to letting it out. We went to bed to the lull of the rivers rumble. My mind raced at first with thoughts of everything to this moment, tomorrow, and missing my daughter. Not wanting to fight my sleep too long with these thoughts I focused on my breath. I love watching the breath of The Universe move into and through my body. After a few deep breaths my thoughts were hushed out along with the rumble of the river by by the nights stillness. I was ready to relinquish my self to the realm of dreams, excited for the eclipse, I danced between realms before fully surrendering.

The Long Road Home
* * *

You can go into the darkest room full of the most hatred, anger, and fear with the tiniest light and the darkness flees. But you can never do the opposite. You can never go into a well light room full of love, appreciation, and gratitude with any amount of darkness and have any effect.
In the face of light the darkness will always flee.

CHAPTER SEVEN

Eclipsing the Trip

Day Six: 08/21/2017

My eyes sprang open with excitement for the day. Like the old paper, roll-up blinds, when you pull them and they snap up and spin around a few times. I was thrust from the dream state like I had been pushed from a cliff. I pushed the sleeping bag off me my body and was instantly jolted awake as the cool morning air kissed my skin that was still warm from the cocoon of my hammock. My instant instinct was to lay back down and snuggle up but there was nothing about this day that made me want to lay back down. Poking my head out from under the tarp the darkness before dawn still consumed most the sky. The air patiently waiting to be warmed by the sun that was still working it's way above the horizon. I had maybe twenty minutes before the show started. I was the only creature stirring around camp, but I didn't see Andrews fishing pole leaning against the tree. I figured he had gotten up earlier and went up to the lake to fish. I got my stove ready and went about percolating some coffee. I opted to just eat some trail mix for now not wanting to fuss with making breakfast yet. I put the trail mix and my water bottle into my daypack. As I poured the coffee into my mug the steam carried the aroma to my nose - I could taste the coffee already. I figured I would go to the same rock we gazed at stars on to catch the painting as it had a nice view facing east. As I headed over to the rock I realized Andrew would have a nice view from the top of the sunset too. Andrew and I have always enjoyed the beautiful sky paintings offered at the beginning and end of the day. Whenever we go adventuring we find a nice overlook to enjoy them.

    Andrew and I first met in grade school. My good friend and

childhood neighbor went to school with him. I was the outsider from another school welcomed in to a group of friends from the same school. My friendship with Andrew grew in the later years, after high school. A shared love of recreational activities brought us together. He introduced me to disc-golf and was the first friend I was able to find to go backpacking with me. He is an amazing soul, full of love and drive. As I said before he is stellar at researching things, usually finding our trips for backpacking reading reviews of places. He found us the spot for the eclipse on Google Earth. Rob and I met through Andrew, also sharing a love of recreational activities. He is a fun loving soul always smiling and full of love. He strums on a guitar real nicely - making me wish I brought my guitar every time we're hanging out by the fire. Maranda and I are also connected through Andrew. I only met her when they started dating, just short of ten years ago. She is great and usually stomps along on our backpacking adventures. She is a bright soul and usually plays the mom role and keeps us boys in line when we get wild in nature. They are all some of the most amazing souls I know, all modest in their mindset. Sitting here with the sun about to rise and only a few hours from the eclipse made me realize how blessed I am to be experiencing this with them.

Experiences are the ticks on the clock's face that give meaning and sustenance to life as we spiral through time. The only knowledge that can be glimpsed lies in the experiences we have. Our self can never be defined through these experiences, most of them out side our force. We define our self by how we react to the experiences we have. It either shades your light through fear and hate or it radiates your light through love and appreciation.

The master painter was just laying the first strokes of color onto the canvas. The view looking down into the valley was a work of art in its own right. Mountains poured down on either side of the pass the trail traversed, creating a forbidding stone wall on either side, converging to the back where they peak. The pass opened up to the valley and meadows below. Mountains also formed a wall on the distant horizon across the valley. You could follow the river down the mountain until it cut through the valley and around a bend to the right. Off in the distant sky a hawk soared across cutting through the orange and red colors painting the sky. I closed my eyes and imagined the view the hawk had as he soared over top on another plane. As I took in a few deep breaths I heard something approaching from behind. I turned my head to see Andrew coming down from the lake - fishing pole in hand. He came and sat down while we took a few puffs from the pipe I had in my pocket. He mentioned he had a dope view of the sunrise up top and figured I would be down here enjoying it. He came down ready for breakfast. We sat over there for about fifteen minutes while the painting was finished as we extinguished the pipe.

Heading back over toward camp Rob was out of his tent starting his day and filling his water bottle. I realized I was hungry too and went over to get our food bag down. Maranda was getting out of the tent as I returned with our food bag. Andrew mixed up some dank (delicious/extremely good) egg casserole type backpacking breakfast. Mixing dehydrated eggs, potatoes, cheese and some spices in a ziplock bag. You just add hot water and mix it around. We brought along bacon bits to add for a little extra flavor, if desired. We were all busy talking about the eclipse and what we expected or hoped for. Brief pauses in the conversation allowed enough time to get a bite down here and there before the conversation carried on. The mountain atmosphere was bubbling over with a noticeable excitement that was felt around camp.

After we finished breakfast and cleaned up from it we decided to hike up to the lake in about a half hour to enjoy one last view before the eclipse. We were only a few hours away from the eclipse. Andrew and Maranda snuck into their tent to get ready and Rob snuck into his to roll a joint or two out of the wind. I took the time to go over to one of the rocks sitting out into the water, on the edge, to get some water for filtering while enjoying the moment. We went about getting a couple snacks and water bottles in order for our hike up to the lake before hanging the food bags up. As we broke the protection of shade, offered by the bank of trees we were camped under, we stepped out onto the trail and began the ascent. The sky was clear and the sun was moving toward it's peak as we moved toward the mountain's peak. Reaching our destination we found some nice boulders on the top ridge of rocks to sit atop and gaze down on the lake. More people had filtered in at some point, most of them day hiked up here for the eclipse, the number of camps was about the same. The sun and wind blowing off the lake offered a near perfect mix of warmth from the sun and coolness from the breeze. Basking in the rays we marveled at how blessed we were with perfect weather for this trip and eclipse. A palpable energy swirled around like the wind that broke the surface of the lake into choppy waves. After about thirty minutes of enjoyment we were ready for camp again and allowed the wind to push us off the peak. With only a couple hours before the eclipse we scurried down the mountain with excitement.

Under the shade from the grove of trees at camp Maranda and Andrew relaxed in the hammock together, Rob went into his tent to get organized, and I headed over to get the food bags down to retrieve some snacks. I went back to sit down as I was on a mission specialized in acquiring beef jerky. Reaching in my arm disappeared into the bag from the elbow down. I felt like I was on an agreeable version of the old tv show Fear Factor, feeling around in the dark bag with my fingers. I wanted to find the treat without pulling everything out. Finally I hit pay dirt and pulled my hand up with my treasure. When the bag of jerky emerged from the bag s small bit of aluminum foil came with it. It was folded, fairly neatly and purposeful, not crumpled like trash. I was captivated by it and began unfolding it to see what it contained. Once the last fold was undone I held the aluminum like a neatly folded treasure map in my hand. A beam of sun that broke though the trees was reflected in the middle. Right beside the beam of light were three equally cut pieces of paper. (I could almost hear the heavenly harps strumming). It appeared to be LSD, maybe and maybe not based off previous experience. The food bag was in my possession the entire trip and I never noticed it. Even after dumping out the contents to find something earlier in the trip did not unearth the treasure. I quickly went about the detective work to ascertain where it came from, questioning all my companions. Maranda was essentially ruled out before the investigation began. No one would confess to the act and we were left with a cold case. Perhaps it was just a gift from The Universe. Andrew, Rob, and I went about disposing of the evidence. Maranda it seemed would be taking on the role of "camp mom" ensuring the childish boys were in no harm. We had about a half hour before the moon started to break across the face of the sun when the experiment began. I packed a small bowl to commemorate the occasion.

After our paper treats were consumed we rehung the food bags. Maranda handed out the eclipse glasses and we grabbed our chairs and water bottles to head over to watch the eclipse at what has became our lookout spot, the outcropping of rocks across the trail from camp. We sat back chattering with excitement for what was to come. The birds were matching pitch and pace with their songs. It seemed they were just as excited for the moment. Energy reverberated out in bubbles, pushing the limits of whatever membrane contained it, to the breaking point. This was the first eclipse we would experience in totality. I had witnessed an eclipse in grade school, I believe it was just a partial but I have glimpses of memories of it that make me think it might of been a total. Either way this was the first one I was going to totally soak in and experience. We brimmed with excitement for what was about to unfold we bubbled over in cascades. Everyone had a smile consuming their face with love and joy. The eclipse was already an amazing and energetic experience and the magic was yet to begin.

Andrew announced that we had nine minutes until the beginning I noticed the butterflies taking up residence in my belly. They're usually a precursor to the effects of the LSD experience kicking in. Based on everyones mood, I didn't need to ask, everyone was on the same level as me. Things were getting ready to take off and I could no longer contain my excitement in a chair. I stood up and opened my arms wide with gratitude to The Universe before moving around for a bit. It turned out to be building into dance as the excitement of everything pulled me. Looking at everyone I imagined what a sight we were for any thing looking down on us. They were all sitting in their chairs gazing at the sun with their eclipse glasses on, cardboard frames with plastic lenses that are mirrored from the outside but tinted when looking through with them on. And here I was dancing with two left feet. I decided I had to join the crowd and slipped my glasses on to gaze toward the ball of fire in the sky. The moon was just beginning to eclipse the sun as the LSD was just starting to eclipse my periphery - in perfect timing.

The trip up the mountain to see the eclipse was like a outward reflection of the trip taken inward to get here to witness the eclipse, everything was coming to a zenith here on the mountain during the peak of an eclipse. I was soaking in the whole experience with the last bits of un-eclipsed rays of sunshine radiating down on my face with a blast of energy so intense I could feel it. The wind was swirling around me, cooling me off as it blew across my face and whooshing past my ears. It was rushing past like moments in time that sweep me away and carry me to bliss. I was merely a leaf being carried away on the universal winds to where I was needed. I was floating along the line of real and surreal and the two were becoming intertwined. It was becoming unfeasible to distinguish between the two. I have had many times my dreams felt like real life and moments in real life that felt so good I thought I might be dreaming. This fell into one of those categories.

The Long Road Home

I was wallowing in this joy with the effects of a foreign, but familiar, substance running through me. The moon was moving across the sun for what seemed like an eternity. The more it covered it's face the more I was driven to dance. Before I embarked on this adventure when any one would ask where I was going I would tell them "I'm going to dance on the side of a mountain in the totality of an eclipse." Here I was dancing on the side of the mountain almost in totality of the eclipse. We were all beaming with joy as the moon moved further across the sun, covering it more and more with each moment. The bubbles of excitement were about to burst.

As the sun was totally eclipsed by the moon the entire range was filled with a momentary stillness. Silence overtook as everything seemed to stop and take in the moment. After a few moments that seems to stretch into eternity the silence was broken by a unanimous "whoa" and every one ruptured with joyous love. I punctuated the excitement with a howl that dwarfed the one I had let out in the meadow yesterday. It echoed around the mountain a few times. After a couple moments I heard the howls being reflected back from others around the mountains. The excitement was resonating through the mountains as an odd light radiated throughout the air. It was like a dawn/dusk mixed with day and night - an odd and unreal essence I have trouble describing - it left all your senses bewildered. Time seemed to stop but totality would only last a few moments before the sun's light would begin to peer back through the other side of the eclipse. Breaking through the darkness and filling the air with light. Everyone could feel the strangeness that accompanied the moment - even Maranda mentioned she felt a weirdness - we were all apparently on the same level. We stayed on the outlook for about an hour after the eclipse soaking in the excitement of the moment and digesting the emotions. Someone broke a joint out that we sparked to celebrate totality and let everything marinate. People were already making their descent down the mountain as we headed back to camp.

We found a rock on the water that allowed all of us to sit comfortably and enjoyed the sound of the water rushing. Amongst the chatter and excitement the joint from earlier entered the picture - celebratory fireworks for the excitement of the day were in order. Andrew and Maranda headed over to make some lunch but neither Rob or I were ready to eat so we stayed by the water and finished the snacks. While Andrew and Maranda got lunch ready the idea was brought about to go up and enjoy the lake for a bit after eating. I loaded up some snacks and my water bottle into my daypack after the joint was extinguished and switched out my sandals for my hiking boots. Up at the lake the rocks were almost empty now aside from a few sparse tents dotting the land. Even with less people the energy radiating around the lake was just as powerful and magical. A majority of the people were basking in the sun atop the rocks but a couple groups of people were hanging out down by the waters edge. A few brave souls even conquered the gelid glacial melt waters for a brief dip. We worked our way down the various levels of rocks and cliffs making our way to the waters edge. None of us had any intentions of dipping anything more than a toe in today. We found a nice flat rock jutting out into the lake about 6 inches above the water where we sat down and enjoyed the views and the sun. The winds that fueled the choppy waves on the water were calm today and the water looked more like a reflecting pool. Other than a few fish jumping here and there the surface was as smooth as glass. We sat on the rock and enjoyed the views from the lake, tucked into the mountains, before we decided to head back to camp. The sun was scorching on the exposed rock and we sought the fragments of shade offered by the small grove of trees we were camped under. We took a quick hit from the pipe and headed back down the mountain.

Today would be relaxing day, full of sitting around camp and hanging out in the shade. The hammock near the water would be put to good use with plenty of naps. Maranda went over and sat on a rock by the water and read for a little bit and Rob and Andrew were sitting down enjoying the relief of the shade trees. I headed out to roam around the mountain near camp and perused the area for any small rocks that might catch my eye. Most of the rocks I've found to collect or wrap into necklaces have been obtained along adventures. I found a few nice rocks before retreating from the sun and heading back to camp. I could here the faint sound of bluegrass playing through Andrews speaker connected to his phone. I danced my way to camp as I followed the song back. Andrew and Rob were still relaxing in the shade and Maranda was still on the rock reading her book. I grabbed the beef jerky from the food bag and headed over to the shade. The conversation danced between how amazing the eclipse was and plans for the next couple days.

I was pulled away from the group, at some point, to go down and sit on a rock by the water. I felt the need to go and meditate by the waters as my thoughts floated down with the current. About 50 yards down the mountain from camp I found the perfect rock sitting near the waters edge. There was a view, through a couple tall pines that sat twenty feet or so in front of me about ten feet apart. I could watch the water cut a way down the mountain and disappear off into the valley. I could see the entire valley down below and the mountains off in the distance. It was magical. I sat here letting my thoughts move as they do while focusing on my breath as the water battered the rocks near me. My mind was continually pulled toward my daughter, who I missed immensely at this point. The last couple days of not being able to communicate with her have affected me more than I realized. It was almost a week since seeing her beautiful smile and nearly two days since talking to her. She was the one who first thrust me into this adventure in to self. While I needed this portion of the journey on my own, to be alone and find my self, I wanted her here with me to experience everything I was. This was the longest we had been apart from each other ever and I had not prepared for the choppy waters. After a few moments of being flushed with thoughts of her it felt like the waters from the river were washing over me. The feeling of missing her were becoming overwhelming and I began to weep uncontrollably. They were not only tears of sorrow or sadness though, many were filled with love and gratitude for everything I had been blessed with. It felt like I had been thrown into the river and the waters were rushing over me. It was refreshing to experience the feeling of letting your emotions wash over and flow through you. Just as the ducts were closing off and drying up I decided it felt nice to get up and stretch my body. I intended to go back to camp and regain my space in the group with a fresh bowl of cannabis.

    I gave love, thanks, and appreciation for the space I had just occupied and turned around to head back to camp. As I turned I looked down and spotted a flower about five feet below me. A sole flower growing out of a rock with four vibrantly purple pedals symmetrically spaced. The stalk was thin and wiry as it bent its way up toward the sun - using all its strength to keep the flower from falling over. I had this immense feeling that this flower was blooming for me so I went down to sit with it for a bit. Sitting amongst boulders and debris from what appeared to be flood washout it stuck out like the moon in the night sky. A seed of beauty growing amid the chaos that pervaded the space. I felt a connection with the flower's ability to bring harmony and beauty out of chaos if we can focus on the light and radiate our love. It was a reminder from The Universe of the beauty available if focus on love and light is maintained. I felt this flower was here for me, to show me love and beauty amid the uproar of my emotions. It was a sign to continue moving toward the light no matter where you find your self. I felt like I was wrapped in an embrace of loving understanding from a source I could only sense and never see directly - Source. Moments like this are how it presents itself and communicates with me. I sat down beside the flower as our energy danced together. Conversing and sharing our love and gratitude together. I kneeled closer so I could take in its sweet fragrance. With the first sniff I got mostly petal so I altered my position and centered in, taking it the sweet aroma with gratitude. I felt blessed to be immersed in this experience. I sat with it a few moments more before offering it love and heading back to camp. I made my way up to the rock I sat on and mediated just moments before and looked out at the valley below. My heart was overflowing with love and appreciation for being. I let the water carry that love and appreciation out into the world.

Directing a farewell bit of loving energy toward my flower friend I turned to head back to camp and enjoy a different type of flower with my friends. Just as I got turned around Andrew and Rob were walking toward me, about ten yards away, laughing down the mountain. When they got to the rock Rob extended his hand holding a pipe filled with a bright green bunch of cannabis, offering me the first hit. Explaining they were sitting over at camp and figured I could use a fresh pipe. I laughed and told them I was just coming over to smoke with them. We were all dancing together in harmony with The Universe. Once the bowl of flowers was sparked my mind floated back to my flower friend. I beamed with excitement as I told them about the flower and the things I have experienced over here. I told them to fully take in the glory of the rock blossoming out of the rock we should go smell it, telling them about its sweet smell. Mind you, I was a giggling mess with everything going on and telling them about my conversations with the flower. Rob, who was fully immersed in the moment and held no reservations, was delighted with the idea of taking in its fragrance and kneeled down to take in the aroma. I could sense that Andrew, a more analytical soul, held reservations about it. I could tell he thought I was pranking him or something. He didn't say anything but I could sense it. I kneeled down beside the flower and took in a deep breath of the beautiful fragrance to show him I am sincere. He kneeled down and hesitantly took in a small breath and mentioned that it smelled good. I could tell that he only smelled the petal and did not get the full fragrance of the flower, as I did the first time. I did not push any more as by this point we were all laughing hysterically, bubbling over with joy. In life the same is true, if we hesitantly bask in the glory of the moment and only partially smell the flower in fear we will never fully realize the beauty the moment offers us - even through the chaos. We made our way up to the rock I sat on and thought of my daughter while we finished the bowl and soaked in the views down the valley. We seemed to be working our way back toward camp.

Back at camp Maranda, who had been sitting by the water reading, made her way back over to the group of chairs. Her and I seem to share a love for sitting near the waters edge. While we sat the idea was brought up of going up to the lake for the sunset. We all agreed it sounded like a great plan, we still had a few hours until it set. We discussed our plans for the next days hike off the mountain and driving up to Grand Teton National Park. In the midst of the conversation I realized I only had a few days until I headed back to Dayton to see my daughter. I was bursting with joy for this next adventure back to her. I was filled with as much, if not slightly more joy than before I left to come on this journey. It never stopped me from enjoying the moment and may have helped me enjoy being here with them more thoroughly.

Rob and I decided we were finally ready to eat some food and retrieved our food bag to look at our options. I let him pick what he wanted to eat while I went to get some water to boil and put it on the stove. After we finished dinner we cleaned up and decided to head up to the lake. We still had about an hour before the sun set but were uncertain if we would make it back up to the lake in the morning and we wanted to enjoy it beforehand. I grabbed some beef jerky and trail mix to throw in my daypack and we hung the food bags and filled our water bottles up. Once everything at camp was put away we headed up to the lake. The new joke had become comparing how "clipsy" things were (how much they resembled and reminded us of our brief time in totality). We agreed the sky on the horizon fit that description perfectly. We all laughed with love for the perfection and joy of this day. We were soaked in the last bits of sun while soaking in the last bits of solace the lake offered - even through the laughter. After about a half hour the sun was starting to work its way over the horizon and paint the sky with beautiful hues of pink, red, and purple. I packed up a pipe to enjoy while we took in the moment. The sky was immaculate, only a couple wispy clouds were on the horizon to the west, adding a layer for the color to penetrate. The only camp that remained around the lake was on the peninsula in the middle of the lake. The smoke from their fire danced up into the sky. It all reflected off the mirrored stillness of the lake. Once the last strokes were being dispersed we decided we were all about ready to head back down to camp. We snapped a couple pictures to remember the moment and scurried back down the mountain toward camp.

At camp we decided to start a fire as the air was getting a quick chill. The temperatures were dropping with the sun over the horizon as we all retreated to our sleeping quarters to change into warmer clothes for the rest of the night. It was probably in the mid fifties, a drastic change from the near triple digit heat of the day. Sitting in the presence of the fire, as it crackled and popped, we reminisced about living through the experience of being in totality during an eclipse. Reliving the experience through memories recorded in the mind like reels of tape. Through the commotion of conversation and laughter Andrew pulled out his phone to share something from earlier. He had recorded a video of the eclipse with his phone laying on the ground pointed at the sun. Our conversations and laughter could be heard in the background. We laughed uncontrollably as I was heard in the background of the recording saying, "Put me here for-fucking-ever." A moment that had slipped into the abyss of joy that was today I packed a pipe of cannabis and handed it off for someone else to start the rotation. It helped kick in a subtle feeling from our experiment earlier in the day.

At some point someone noticed the stars were out magnificently bright as they peered out through the trees and suggested going to the lookout point to gaze out. We all looked up and agreed it was a great idea. We grabbed our water bottles and headed across the trail. The last vestiges of light on the horizon from dusk gave way to the darkness of night. The stars were out in full force with sparkling lights scattered across the sky. The Milky Way was radiant enough to seemingly cast a shadow, again. We were all exhausted from the day but energized from the activities at the same time. After every one got to see a shooting star or two we decided to head back to the fire and wind down for the night.

After around thirty minutes Maranda headed off to the warmth and comfort of bed. Rob pulled out one last joint and offered it up as a closing celebration to the day. Andrew and I delightfully agreed that the day deserved celebration. We threw one last piece of wood on the fire and put some bluegrass on low volume, just loud enough to hear over the roar of the water. Once the joint was finished we grabbed the last snacks out for the night before hanging up the food bags. Coming back to watch the fire burn down to embers before we filled up our water bottles and Andrew headed to bed. Rob and I stayed up around an hour longer watching the embers flash in and out of existence while we relived the moments from today that seemed to flash out of time. We took a couple more puffs from a pipe before dousing the embers with water. We were both exhausted from the day and ready for bed. It was a perfect night for sleeping. It was clear, I could see stars sticking out of the sky from under my tarp. A breeze pushed the cool air under my tarp as the river lulled me to sleep.. I fell asleep with my sleeping bag at my feet.

Amid the turmoil you can choose to live in fear or you can choose to live in love.
The situation is not yours but the choice is.

CHAPTER EIGHT

Peaks of the Tets

Day Seven: 08/22/2017

My eyes popped open, like two kernels of corn when the steam inside builds beyond the membranes ability to contain it, with the need to go pee. The chill in the morning air hit my face like a bat as my arms drew in toward my body in an attempt to hold on to the warmth from my cocoon. I wanted to pull my sleeping bag over my head and fully retreat to its warm embrace but I caught glimpse of the eastern horizon from under my tarp. The very first rays of morning light were just peeking over the edge of the world. I reached into the gear sling, a smaller hammock hanging under my hammock holding most of my gear off the ground, and searched for my lightweight thermals. I slid them on under my shorts and slipped into my boots and out of the hammock. Andrew's pole was with him at the lake fishing while Rob and Maranda were still resting peacefully. I grabbed some trail mix from the food bag and hung it back up. With snacks and water in hand I headed over to our look out rock. Just as I broke into the openness from the grove of trees I noticed Andrew coming down the trail. He took his pole over to camp and came to watch the sun rise with me. Other than the peace fishing offers him he had no luck fishing today. I sarcastically offered him a puff from the pipe to take the pain away. He laughingly obliged, joking that while he couldn't catch a fish maybe he could catch a buzz. The sky was filled with a bright red as the sun burned its way over the horizon. Across the valley the mountains were painted gold as the morning sun kissed them. As the sun reached higher into the sky and washed away the colors it had just painted Andrew and I headed over to camp. We'd start to break down camp and prepare for the hike down shortly. We wanted an early start to the day as we had a lot planned. Just as we got down from the rock we could see Rob just poking his head out of his tent.

While Maranda caught a bit more sleep we started to break down camp. Andrew gathered and packed what he could while Rob and I got our tent and hammock taken down and our backpacks mostly packed. We left the top space in our packs open to stash the food and eating supplies after breakfast. I headed over to the river to get some water to filter just as Maranda was getting out of the tent. She said we didn't wake her up though she may have just been being kind. We sat around and ate some breakfast as we enjoyed the last moments of relaxation at camp. When everything from breakfast was cleaned up, after Andrew and Maranda finished packing their backpacks, we smoked a small pipe, our ceremonial way to break camp. With packs on we turned to look over camp to make sure nothing was left. You could barely tell we were there. We disappeared out of the trees and into the open, down the trail.

Hiking down the mountain was slightly easier, although in steep sections your toes can get smashed in the front of your boots. We made pretty good time with a decent pace only stopping for short breaks to hydrate or moments when the views were too good. The views were in front of you nearly the whole time down the mountain so stopping to soak them in was not as necessary. Rob outpaced us all down the mountain, jogging most the time. I had never seen anyone jog down a mountain with a backpack full of gear and I am not sure I ever will again. The three of us were in no rush and only broke the pace of a walk on steep sections that forced our hand - or feet. We had keys for both cars so Rob was not going any further than the trail head with out us. We passed through a grove of trees and the trail bent around to the right in a subtle and ninety-degree bend and dropped sloped a rock face. After turning the bend you could see the field where we parked off in the distant valley. Most of the cars had left, only a small fraction remained. Only a couple cars dotted the green fields now. It was still a couple miles out but their sight re-energized me for the remaining portion down the mountain. The cars were the size of ants from our view but our excitement to get there was the size of an elephant. We still hadn't caught up to Rob. We were all pretty exhausted from the past couple days events. The hike down in the open heat of the sun did not offer any respite. We all wondered how

Rob was running, and why he was. We took one last break at the site of the cars and decided not to stop again in hopes of making good time. They needed to stop in Dubois for gas and hopefully some lunch too after we got to the car. Leaving out from there to drive north to Grand Teton National Park to set up camp before leaving for Yellowstone National Park. We heading there today to see the Grand Prismatic Spring and Old Faithful as Maranda had these on her bucket list.

Rob had taken up refuge on a wooden rail fence near the trail head. We met up with him and started the mile or two hike down the road to the cars. When we finally reached the cars we couldn't get our packs off our backs quickly enough. After dropping our packs we quickly opened the doors to release the hot, stale air that pervaded the interior of our cars. I popped open the tailgate on my CR-V and curiously opened my cooler. It had been sitting in a hot car in the sun for 2 days and I wondered how cold it would be. As I cracked the lid open I was happy to see the last relics of ice floating in ice-cold water. I reached my hand in and pulled out a gatorade for each of us. Everyone relished in an ice cold drink after a hike down the mountain in the hot sun. We decided to pack some cannabis in a pipe to celebrate the hike down the mountain and next leg of the journey. After all the snacks were consumed we loaded the cars and headed back down the road. The dirt road leading back to the main road was filled with ruts and the drive was slow. Before too long we were turning left on the main road to head back to Dubois.

When we pulled into town we parked along the main street before getting gas and walked down the street hoping to find a place to eat. It was a fruitless venture for food here though. There were three restaurants in town - two were not open for the day yet and the other had an hour plus wait for a seat. We found a coffee shop before heading back to the cars. On the way back we passed a quant little meat shop we hadn't noticed before. Andrew and Rob went in and purchased some hotdogs to cook on the fire tonight and some little sausage snack things for our hike tomorrow. It was a nice walk through town. The sidewalks were wood plank with folks shuffling between shops and enjoying the day. It was not surprising that the buildings all held an old western aura. I imagine a majority of the buildings here were original to when the town was originally established. We settled on stopping for gas before going about our search for lunch and headed to the only gas station on the edge of

The Long Road Home

town. As it worked out a small BBQ stand was tucked in just behind the gas station. It looked and smelled like the small building offered big taste. It was probably a twenty foot by twenty foot building with outdoor seating at picnic tables under the shade of an awning. A lovely and friendly couple, maybe in their sixties, from Texas ran the stand. He made his own sauces, naturally, and handled smoking the meats. She made the deserts and the side dishes. Their team work seemed effective and efficient. They were happy with a noticeable love for life. You could taste the love they put into preparing the food. After enjoying the food and the shade we headed back to our cars.

We headed down the road with tanks full of gas and stomachs full of delicious food. I even got a refill of the sweet tea from the stand. I normally make the sweet tea my grandma used to make as a kid and drink that but this was a refreshing change of pace. It was a beautiful drive to the park filled with lovely scenery on either side the whole way. After maybe an hour or two we the scenery shifted and took a majestic turn when the Grand Teton Mountain Range came into view. I had been following them the whole way here and paid more attention to the scenery than the time or direction. The mountains were jutting out above the horizon making any mountains or cliffs before them seem like hills. The longest and only strenuous part of the drive was entering the gates and driving through the park to camp. There were hoards of crowds and the road was packed.

Jenny Lake Campground is where we would rest for the night. Once we found our spot we quickly acquired some fire wood and set up our tents. After everything was set up and we relaxed for about a half hour we all loaded into their car and headed up to Yellowstone National Park. It's a beautiful park but the main attractions, which are the only thing we came for were unfortunately tourist traps. Walking down a board walk in a congested crowd is not something I generally seek out. We checked out the Grand Prismatic Spring and Old Faithful - I could of dealt without the chaos but the features were beautiful and worth seeing. Before leaving the park we stopped at my favorite attraction, hands down. Inside the general store near Old Faithful we found an ice cream stand. Along with the delicious treat we got some veggies to cook with dinner, some beer, and a couple gifts from the store. We were all more hungry than the ice cream could hold over and didn't waste much time before heading back to camp to cook dinner. My hunger for seeing my daughter was also reaching it's breaking point. I had tried to call her mothers phone to speak to her when I had reception but areas of reception were hit or miss and I was unable to get through.

Originally we planned to do a couple hikes around Yellowstone tomorrow. After seeing Grand Tetons and Yellowstone in the same day and comparing them we were leaning towards doing a longer hike in Grand Tetons and avoiding Yellowstone. On the drive back to camp I had decided if we did the Yellowstone hikes I would skip them and leave to head home and see my daughter. However, I would stay if we stayed in Grand Teton National Park.

Back at camp we didn't waste any time getting a fire started and dinner prepped for cooking. There was a grill grate attached to the fire ring at the camp site which made cooking much easier. Once the fire was hot enough we started cooking the hotdogs on one half of the grate. On the other half we put the vegetables with olive oil and spices in a frying pan. While we waited for the food to cook we smoked a small bowl and discussed options for our hikes tomorrow. Not too much discussion was needed to decide if it would be in Yellowstone or Grand Teton as none of us were very keen on going back up to Yellowstone. Instead the conversation focused on options for hikes around Grand Teton - what each one offered and how difficult it would be. We settled on the hike up to Hidden Falls which wasn't overly difficult but offered plenty of beauty. I resolved to stay around for the hike and leave after. They would stay another night and head down to Denver the next morning to fly home. Dinner finished cooking just as we finished discussing our options and settled on a plan.

After dinner we walked down by the lake to find a spot to watch the sunset. We found an opening in the trees with a log laying down, perfect for sitting, looking west. We lit up a joint to enjoy and celebrate the last sunset we would enjoy together on this trip. As the sun dropped over the horizon it threw hues of orange and red across the sky in an attempt to share its radiance a little longer. The colors reflected off the lake as it undulated from the gentle breeze that pushed across its surface. Off in the distance you could hear a family bubbling with joy and laughter. Our conversations oscillated between the beauty around us and the magic of the eclipse, still. We could find something in every moment that would remind us of the eclipse. It never jaded us from enjoying the moment fully, but rather may have enhanced it with the connection to that magical time. As the sun disappeared below the horizon the bugs, mainly mosquitos, came out

The Long Road Home

from hiding - they were making it hard to enjoy the moment fully. Before the final strokes of paint were laid we extinguished the joint as it was finishing and made quick work back to camp.

At camp we quickly scrambled in to our tents to put on long sleeve shirts and pants to ward off the mosquitos. One or two of them applied a little bug spray to their exposed skin as well but I passed on that option, relying on the protection longer layers offered. The coals of the fire from dinner were still warm which made starting the fire again simple. We laid a couple logs in the ring with some kindling below and between them. With the help of a fat wood fire starter it was roaring again quickly. Once the fire was crackling with consistency and did not need tending I snuck away to my car. Everyone was joyously surprised when I returned with the cache of supplies for s'mores. Through patches of open sky between the trees above we gazed out at the few stars visible in our small window. Our conversation crackled with the fire while we enjoyed our fireside snacks.. I snuck over to the picnic table and packed a small pipe of cannabis to enjoy once we were finished snacking on s'mores. When the logs were about consumed we put a couple more logs on the fire as Maranda was getting ready for bed. When she finally retreated to the tent, for rest, we put two small pieces of wood on the fire as our nightcap. We enjoyed a couple beers while we smoked the pipe of cannabis and watched the fire dance. In the glow of the fire we all took note when a pair of headlights pulled into the camp beside us, near my tent. A younger couple got out and started setting up their tent. Once the fire had consumed the last piece of wood we lasted long enough to watch the embers flash in and out of existence momentarily. We were all ready to flash out for the night and doused the embers with water before storing everything in either our locked cars or the bear proof box at camp.

With camp cleaned up and everything put away we headed to our tents for bed. The couple who had set up amidst the glow of our fire were being loud. Thankfully I packed my earbuds for my phone. I stuffed them in my ears and and let the calming melodies of Jack Johnson lull me quietly. I set a timer so the music would stop after a couple hours and closed my eyes. His music always puts me in a good mood and I am fairly certain I dozed off with a smile on my face.

"A dream you dream alone is only a dream. A dream you dream together is a reality."

David Brown
~ *John Lennon*

CHAPTER NINE

The Long Road Home

Day Eight: 08/23/2017

I was yanked awake by a squirrel barking from one of the trees just outside the tent. I tried to roll over for a little more sleep when it quieted down for a moment. The moment I would close my eyes it started again. After a few rotations of this game I sat up out of my sleeping bag and unzipped the door of my tent to enter the world. Andrew and Maranda were already out of their tent, Rob would be out shortly. Andrew had gotten up before everyone, as usual, and saw a small red fox running through camp when he went to the bathroom. He spotted it a couple more times when he got back to camp as it rummaged around for food. The squirrel barking from the tree was upset by his presence and warning other squirrels in the area about the fox. The tree he was barking from was directly outside Andrew and Marandas tent and the limb he perched on was right above it. She was awaken by the chatter about a half hour before I was. Off on the eastern horizon you could see the last few splotches of color being strewn through the sky. We quickly went about making some coffee and eating breakfast before getting ready for the day. Once we cleaned up we loaded some snacks and water bottles into our daypacks and loaded into the car to head out for our hike.

We wound our way down the road through the park to the trailhead. We had roughly an hour drive through the park to get there. The wildlife seemed to be just getting the day started too. Bunnies and birds were scurrying around in the morning sun. The wildflowers were just turning their heads back toward the sun and opening up for the day, exposing their beauty, searching out the warmth of the sun.

David Brown

As we came around a bend in the road something big was crossing the road about a hundred yards ahead of us. Initially, we got excited and thought it was a moose but also thought it might be an elk. We stopped to get a couple pictures. We were in awe of the beauty the park offered.

When I was a teenager in high school I had the opportunity to go to Germany for a month with our student exchange program. That trip opened my eyes to the amount of beauty and magic the world had to offer. Since then I have always wanted to go back and explore more of Germany and Europe . It started a fire of desire to get out of my region and explore the world. Germany made it evident that I was not content with staying in Ohio. This trip has opened my mind to the beauty the Western US has to offer - even in this little sliver I was exploring. My cup has overflowed with awe and appreciation for the beauty unfolding before me at each turn in the journey. Each moment has showed me a new aspect of beauty in a new way.

The doors of the car sprang open as soon as the car was in the parking space. We all excited the car with excitement to both get out of the car to stretch and start our hike in the woods. On our way to the trailhead we passed the park gift shop and decided to stop back after our hike so I can look for a souvenir for my daughter. When we came to the lake we followed the edge for a short distance then crossed over a wood plank bridge leading to the trailhead. There was another boardwalk off the bridge leading to a small shack on the edge of the lake that offered canoe, kayak, and small motor boat rentals. They also offered a ferry service to a trailhead on the other side of the lake. Our trail wound around on the other side and followed the edge of the lake. The trail climbed the mountain on the other side of the lake on a gravel path. There were a decent amount of people on the trail but everyone was separated enough that it didn't feel congested. We wouldn't leave the side of the mountain that overlooked the lake until we got toward the top. At the beginning of the trail there were a few spots to get off the trail and walk to the waters edge, about a hundred feet from the trail. Before we got too high up the mountain we found one that had a beautiful pebble beach leading into the water with a fallen tree about five feet from the water - perfect for sitting and gazing out. We took advantage of the space to enjoy the view for a few moments. The water was clear enough to see the bottom for about twenty feet before the pebbles on the bottom dropped out of sight. On the opposite side the lake passed between two mountains and

The Long Road Home

appeared to disappear into the horizon. The mountains in the backdrop looked like ripples of waves on the water. The view was something I would expect to see on a postcard.

The further up the mountain we got on the trail the more the views of the lake were covered by trees. There were a few spots to stop and rest with breaks in the trees and you could overlook the lake. On one of our breaks, maybe halfway up the mountain, Andrew spotted a bald eagle down near the water. It was probably two hundred yards below us, and while tiny, the white head stuck out as the sun shone upon it. It didn't do justice to the size of it but there was no mistaking the white helmet. I looked over and Rob, moved by the majesty, had his hand over his heart as a tear ran down below his sunglasses, glistening in the sun. We tried snapping a picture but couldn't get a decent one and moved on up the mountain sans a picture. At our final break overlooking the lake, before breaking into the forest, we took advantage of the solitude and peace and packed up a small pipe of cannabis. There was a huge boulder sticking roughly three feet out of the ground and was flat enough on top to sit on.

The view was enough to take your breath away, if the cannabis didn't. The sky was crisp blue with sparse clouds dotting it. There were mountains surrounding the lake as a single motor boat dashed across, nearly cutting it down the middle. Behind it a wake broke off to either side as waves radiated out from the wake and rippled toward the shore. The sun shimmered off the wrinkled surface like a cut gem that catches the light. A couple hawks soared high above us in search of food. Just below us, in the area of the pebble beach we had hung out on, was an area of algae or something that gave the water a radiant green color that stood out against the bright blue water of the lake and matched the colors of the pines above -maybe brighter. We took a couple pictures after soaking up the views and headed back up the mountain. A little further up we moved deeper into the forest. The change in scenery was a welcome change from the open portion of the trail, exposed to the sun, we had just come off of. It was at least ten degrees cooler in the shade. After about twenty or thirty minutes of stumbling down the trail we reached a point that we could hear the roar of waterfall we were headed toward. You may have been able to hear it 100 yards or so earlier if you were a little quieter than we were. The waterfalls were called Hidden falls but based on the number of people on the trail to them someone let the word out. A couple more turns and the trail came to the area of The Hidden Falls.

David Brown

After crossing a small stream we worked through the forest a short way further as the roar of the waterfall grew loader. We came to the river, off to the left, the waterfall was roughly a couple hundred feet up stream. The river below the falls was scattered with giant boulders jutting out off the water, probably carried down the mountain by the water at some point or chipped off from its force. Groups of people hopped across the smaller rocks sticking out of the water and worked their way closer to the waterfall where about a dozen people were already hanging out at the base. People were hanging out on some of the more accessible boulders that were scattered through the water and some kids were splashing around in the water as they played. I worked my way across a few of the smaller rocks to one of the more secluded boulders that was empty. I climbed my way to the top where a smooth, flat table waited for me. I sat on the boulder a couple hundred feet from the falls and enjoyed the moment. I closed my eyes and took a few deep breaths as I let all the sounds dance around me. The atmosphere was roaring with the rumble from the falls filling the air and the joy from the souls filling the voids. Rob took advantage of the break and worked his way closer to the falls. I snapped a couple pictures for him before sliding off the top of the rock and heading back to shore.

After about an hour of hanging out near the falls we decided to work our way back down the mountain. We were open to the idea of taking any side trails that caught our attention. After a short time we came to an opening in the forest holding a meadow full of bright yellow wildflowers blowing in the breeze. A crisp blue sky and a snow-capped mountain in the background each towered above the flowers. I stopped to smell the flowers, soak in the view for a few moments, and snap a couple pictures before scurrying off to catch up with the group. A couple turns in the trail after I reunited with the group we came to a turnoff for Moose Ponds Trail. We took the right and headed down the trail that led around a pond (presumably Moose Pond) and into the forest behind it. It looked like the perfect place to spot a moose. Just as we came to the pond we crossed paths with a family coming from the opposite direction. After exchanging brief greeting they let us know they had just seen a moose on the move about a hundred yards down the trail. Everyone was excited by the prospect of seeing a moose and we hurried down the trail. After soaking in the view for a moment I snapped a couple pictures and tailed the group down the trail. There was a beautiful meadow of

The Long Road Home

wildflowers on the other side of the pond with Teewinot Mountain stretching toward the clouds in the background. Teewinot mountain is the tallest peak in the Teton Mountain Range - a jagged, exposed rock peak.

We marched down the trail as it curved around the pond and escaped deeper into the forest, still following the ponds edge. Our eyes gazed over the landscape as we followed the path. Peering into the underbrush in attempts to see a moose. It was going to be impossible to see a moose in the dense undergrowth unless it wanted to be seen. The trail crossed over a couple small streams with cool glacial water running down the mountain. We stopped at each on for a brief break to enjoy its beauty. I would take advantage of the time to peruse the land for rocks. A couple times we took our boots off and dipped our feet in the water and let the cold race up our legs. We wound our way around the entire trail, only a few miles, with no moose but plenty of other gorgeous sights. AT the other end of the trail dumped us out near the bottom of Hidden Falls Trail by Jenny Lake where the hike had started earlier that day. We stopped off in the park store before loading in the cars to head back to camp. Inside the store we showed the park ranger pictures of the animal crossing the road on the drive earlier that morning. She verified that it was indeed an elk - the moose still eluded us.

As we pulled out of the parking lot and back onto the road my mind began to play through all the magical times I had been offered, not only on the hike but on the whole trip. I was in a dance with The Universe. I would occasionally take the lead, metaphorically, but most the time I let my self be spun at arms length before being pulled back in as The Universe led me through this dance. The dance was filled with magical interactions with lovely souls along the whole way while I roved through beautiful, awe inspiring landscapes. From start to finish the journey has been filled with moments for me to spread my love and appreciation to the world and have it reflected back at me. Conversations with strangers felt like I was rekindling with a lost soul I had known previously. At every turn I felt connected to The Universe, to Source, in constant communication - ringing out in harmony. Every moment offered me a new aspect of the beauty being created and I truly felt like I was an intricate part of manifesting the magic.

Rolling down the road as it traced the shore of the lake we came around a bend and noticed a sign ahead for a restaurant and hotel that sat on the lake. I was snapped back to the car ride out of my thoughts as discussions of whether to stop permeated the car. It had been about six hours since we ate breakfast, around seven in the morning, and we were all starving. We did not deliberate too long.

There was a table available outside on the deck right on the lake. While waiting for our food my phone rang. I glanced down and noticed it was my daughters mother, probably my daughter. I would finally get to talk to her. My joy must have been radiating out of me - Maranda instantly guessed it was my daughter calling. I excused myself and walked away so I would not interrupt anybody's meal. I could see her smile and her voice offered me solace. Her voice brings me more serenity than any moment spent in nature. We have always had a close relationship, forged through many shared loves but especially our love for adventure and nature. While the sadness of not having her with me was overwhelming the joy of knowing we would experience different adventures eased the sadness. Joy burst through the phone when I told her I was heading home in a couple days and we would finally see each other. I hung up the phone and went back up to our table which was now filled with food.

With our bellies full of delicious food we headed down the road to camp. Back at camp I wasted no time getting my tent broke down and everything packed into my car. After packing the car we took a walk down the road to get away from the crowds of people near camp. I pulled out a joint for Andrew, Rob, and I to enjoy and celebrate the end of another amazing adventure. A moment to share in the love, appreciation, and gratitude for each other and The Universe. Our walk ended up taking us down to the waters edge, either consciously or subconsciously. I took the time to soak in the views and the energy one last time while we reminisced the trip. As we finished the joint we extinguished it and departed our lakeside retreat.

I made one last sweep through camp to make sure I had everything. We made sure they had everything they need and that they would be able to take it home on the plane. After everything was in order we exchanged love, appreciation, and well wishes for safe travels home before I loaded into the car. With a toot of love from my horn I pulled away and left my fellow adventurers for the final leg of my journey. I stopped by the gas station about a mile from camp to fill up and grab some ice for my cooler. With my drinks chilled and the fuel tank filled I pulled onto the road for the longest leg of my journey. I was headed from Grand Teton National Park in Wyoming to my home in Dayton,

The Long Road Home

Ohio. I was hoping I could drive straight through. Other than stopping for gas or to use the restroom, which hopefully would be combined together, I was hoping my next stop would be my driveway. It was just before five in the evening when I got my journey started and I had over a thousand miles to go.

Around one of the bends in the road I came to a pull off The Universe was pulling me toward. It looked out over a prairie and in the distance the Teton Mountain Range flanked the far horizon. Low clouds from a thunderstorm that was rolling in danced with the peaks from the range and added another dimension to the scene. I got out and took a couple small puffs from my pipe and extended my arms in embrace with Source. I took a couple pictures of the range before a couple taking in the views and snapping photos beside me offered to take a picture of me with the mountains in the backgroung. Taken back by the random act of loving kindness I accepted their offer as graciously as I could muster amid the excitement. After they snapped a couple shots of me and handed my phone back I asked if they would also like a picture with the mountain in the backdrop but they had a camera with a tripod and already handled that. I thanked them, offering them love and peace, before headed a bit further away to grant each of us some solitude. I soaked in the views for about fifteen more minutes before I felt pulled to move back down the road. The road I was on took me back into Dubois, where I stopped for some gas and coffee. When I went inside to pay I noticed the local weekly paper had a front page story on the eclipse. I figured the others would enjoy them and grabbed three copies when I paid for my goods.

My drive after getting gas in Dubois was again following the winding roads through Wyoming countryside to the highway that would take me home. The views in every direction were uniquely beautiful, as I have grown accustomed to here. I peered out from my car windows with amazement at the dreamscape around me. I was headed for Interstate 80 in the southeast corner of Wyoming to follow along the Colorado border into Nebraska. On drives my mind seems to rotate at the same pace as my engine. I have always enjoyed driving as a time to let my thoughts run free while I sort them out.

At some point driving through Wyoming I realized that as much anticipation and excitement that I had to drive out west before leaving I may have anticipated the drive home, back to my daughter, a little more. Adventures offer great opportunities to go out and find beauty in the world. If we are open and fortunate enough our trek leads inward simultaneously to find the beauty we have hidden away within. Sometimes when you are truly blessed you get the once in a lifetime opportunity to experience an eclipse in totality on the side of a mountain. I have been presented beauty around every bend in the path. It was found in every step I took out into the world and each step was reflected inward as I journeyed deeper into my self. Maybe the beauty to be found in the world was just the beauty I had discovered within my self which was being radiated out. Like shadows cast on the wall as I carry the images of grandeur past the fire that is my internal light. I can never find adequate words or ways to describe my experiences. There is no rendering I could stumble upon that could justify the magnitude of the moments. They live like fragments of stardust in my mind - seemingly insignificant in size but truly the essence of every thing. Through these new experiences I have found that the road home, back to family or familiar, can often be the greatest part of the adventure. I have driven over 4000 miles after leaving Ohio. I passed through nine states - seven of which I visited for the first time. I danced in totality of a solar eclipse on the side of a mountain. I witnessed beautiful sights and souls in every moment along the way. The Universe blessed me with the gift of finding beauty in nature and my self. I anticipated this trip so much for nearly a year before leaving that each day seemed gruelingly long. And I enjoyed every moment of it more than I could of imagined or dreamed. The reward waiting at the end of the long road home supersedes it all. My love and desire for adventure is greater than when I left and my appetite has grown to explore deeper inward and out. I now know that no matter how long the adventure last or how far the road takes you, through all the splendor, the long road home will be the most rewarding part of the adventure. The longer you are away and the further you go the more rewarding the return seems to be.

    A couple hours after leaving the Teton Mountain Range in my rearview mirror I came around a bend in the road and found another pull off spot with a open view of the western horizon. The sun was roughly a half hour away from the horizon when I decided to pull off. The Universe was ushering me off on the long road home with a final masterpiece to end the day. I pulled out my backpacking chair and made some coffee as I patiently waited for the painting to begin in the sky. I grabbed some snacks out of the car and pulled the cooler out to rest my feet on while I sat back and relaxed. This was the last sunset I was being gifted with along the trip. The view was magnificent, again.

The Long Road Home

Prairies of long, blowing grass filled the hills that rolled off into the horizon with the occasional cliff jutting out of the landscape. Bright oranges and reds were being splashed across the sky. Any exposed rock was painted gold with the last rays of light. A breeze pushed the grass over, swirling past my ear with a gentle swoosh. A couple clouds pushed past, soaking up any colors in the sky like a sponge. I took in a few deep breaths of gratitude while I enjoyed the moment. Soon I would cross into Nebraska. I was racing east to find the sun rise in hopes it would fuel my energy and support my fight against the pull of sleep. It was still undecided if the excitement to get home to my daughter would be an energizing factor or an exhausting one. I was here now, with the sunset.

    I poured the last of the coffee into my mug and refilled my tea before loading my chair and cooler into the car. After checking my tire pressure I headed back down the road. I would drive for a couple hours before finding a gas station still open. I knew most stations out west closed up through the night and pulled in, unsure when the next open station would be found. With a full tank and a cup of coffee I was back on the long road home.

    I crossed into Nebraska sometimes just after midnight. Nebraska is a fairly mundane state to drive through so I did not mind moving through at night. My energy levels were still about as full as my tank. I was hopeful I would be able to drive through the night. Without scenery to see as I rolled down the road my mind danced between where I was going and where I had been. Most the focus concentrated on the journey ahead - my excitement to see my daughter was growing with each inch of the path I traversed. The cool night air rushed through the open windows and surged past me. The stars I could see through the windows and amid the headlights were bright. I was going to miss the night skies of the west - everything seems more crisp and clear than back east. After about an hour of driving in Nebraska I noticed a gas station ahead that looked open. I pulled in hoping to get fuel to propel me and coffee to energize me through the night. I turned the radio up to an annoying level when I got back on the highway. I put the air conditioner on and turned the fan to high, leaving the windows open. I could feel my energy dwindling - I was doing anything to help me stay awake and alert. I wanted to find the sun rise with hopes the light would keep me awake until I got home. The excitement of getting home did give me some energy but the reality of being awake for nearly eighteen hours and hiking up a mountain in the heat was taking over.

A couple hours longer and my fuel was just under a half tank, my coffee cup was empty, and my energy was running on fumes. As I passed mile marker 210 I glanced at the dashboard clock. The bright red 3:00 was etched into my mind. I quickly decided I would not be able to make it without sleep. A few moment later I passed another sign from The Universe that pulled me where needed. I pulled into the rest area with plans to get a few hours of sleep before finishing my journey.

I planned to wake up before the sun allowing me to catch one last sun rise if I was fortunate enough. I was headed back reshaped by my experiences. Things would never be the same but then again they never are. As much as things may seem repetitive at times, its only that we haven't garnered the full lesson in the moment. If we can shift our perspective we will cycle back through things we have known and see them in a new light - allowing for new lessons. The more you can open your heart and live in love, the more you elevate your perspective and see more connection. Individual moments seem less momentary as they meld together into one timeless being.

Just be love.

This little light of mine, I'm going to let it shine.

www.ingramcontent.com/pod-product-compliance
Lightning Source LLC
Chambersburg PA
CBHW062146100526
44589CB00014B/1704